The Life
of
JOHN CALVIN

John Calvin, aged about 27, during the time of his visit to Ferrara, Italy, 1536.

The Life
of
JOHN CALVIN

W. J. Grier

The Lord our God be with us, as he was with our fathers:
let him not leave us nor forsake us.
1 KINGS 8:57

THE BANNER OF TRUTH TRUST

THE BANNER OF TRUTH TRUST
3 Murrayfield Road, Edinburgh EH12 6EL, UK
P.O. Box 621, Carlisle, PA 17013, USA

*

First published as articles in the
Irish Evangelical magazine

Previously published in
The Banner of Truth magazine

This edition first published 2012
© James, John and Hunter Grier 2012

ISBN: 978 1 84871 181 5

*

Typeset in 10/13 pt Sabon Oldstyle Figures
at the Banner of Truth Trust, Edinburgh

Printed in the USA by
Versa Press, Inc.,
East Peoria, IL

CONTENTS

FOREWORD

WILLIAM JAMES (JIM) GRIER was born on 18 November 1902 and grew up on a farm in County Donegal. As a Classics student at Queen's University Belfast, he was converted through the witness of a Christian student friend and in a W. P. Nicholson mission meeting. He was a foundation member of the university's Christian Union, and then studied theology under Gresham Machen, Robert Dick Wilson and Geerhardus Vos in Princeton Seminary, New Jersey, 1923-25.

Having learned from Machen of the fight for the Reformed faith within Presbyterianism, he returned for a compulsory year at the Irish Presbyterian College in Belfast and found himself in the same fight for the gospel against unscriptural teaching in the college. After three weeks in the classroom, listening in silence to things he knew were wrong, he began to challenge one of his professors, and later became involved as a witness for the prosecution in an attempt at church discipline. When the charges against this professor were defeated by a 90 percent majority in the church courts, Grier regarded this verdict as a declaration of institutional unorthodoxy by the Church and resigned.

He became one of the founding ministers of the Evangelical Presbyterian Church in Ireland, managed the Evangelical Bookshop in central Belfast, edited the Church's magazine for fifty-three years, and ministered the gospel faithfully in what became the Stranmillis congregation. He was a trustee of the Banner of Truth Trust, co-chairman of the Leicester Ministers' Conference, a founding member of the British Evangelical Council (now Affinity), and served on committees of the Evangelical Fellowship of Ireland and the Evangelical Library in Belfast.

About the *Evangelical Presbyterian* magazine Dr Martyn Lloyd-Jones said this:

> I look forward to its coming month by month with great pleasure. It always seems to me to have the ideal blend as regards matter—theology, devotional element, first-class book reviews, pungent comments on current affairs, biographical material, and choice extracts from the writings of the masters. The industry and versatility of the Editor astound me more and more.

Through the magazine and inter-church relations, Jim Grier was a well-known and enormously respected leader throughout the international Reformed constituency. He retired in 1979 after a ministry of almost fifty-two years and went to be with the Lord on 6 August 1983.

He was the author of many booklets, articles, tracts, Daily Readings and Calendar Notes, his major works being *The Momentous Event* in 1945, *The Origin & Witness of the Irish Evangelical Church* in 1948, and *The Best Books* in 1968. He looked forward to bringing out one more book, a life of Calvin based on some of his magazine articles, but declining mental powers during his retirement prevented this. These articles have been edited in the book which follows.

We his three sons would like to thank Mr Ernest Brown who transcribed them from the magazines, Rev. Jonathan Watson who edited them, and Rev. Iain Murray who inspired their republication.

James, John, and Hunter Grier
Belfast
June 2011

Pont-l'Evêque.

Calvin's house in Noyon.

ONE

THE EARLY YEARS

God having taken me from my originally obscure and humble condition, has reckoned me worthy of being invested with the honourable office of a preacher and minister of the gospel.

S O CALVIN WROTE in 1557, when his thoughts went back to his father's parentage. The Cauvin family (better known to history by its Latinized form 'Calvin') belonged to Pont-l'Evêque, a little village whose stone bridge crossed the river Oise, a couple of miles from Noyon, which it served as a port for the shipping of wine. The location had given the Reformer's grandfather employment as a boatman and a cooper, but by 1480 his son Gérard left the village to seek his fortune in Noyon, the cathedral town which lies some fifty miles northeast of Paris in the Picardy region of France. The son was evidently a shrewd man of affairs and was to prosper with 'many irons in the fire'. Positions involving both ecclesiastical and civil offices were in his hands—as a law agent, procurator-fiscal for the county, secretary of the diocese, and attorney of the cathedral chapter. To these were added his role as a counsellor for clergy and nobility.

The façade of Noyon Cathedral.

Gérard Cauvin's neighbours said he made 'good use of his eyes' when he sought the hand of the beautiful Jeanne Le Franc, daughter of a well-to- do inn-keeper who had come to live in Noyon. To Gérard and Jeanne seven children were born—two sisters and five brothers, but two of the brothers died in infancy. John, the second of the three surviving boys, was born on Tuesday, 10 July 1509. In his childhood he lived under the shadow of the 'long, straight-backed' cathedral of his native town. His devout mother brought up her children in all the rites and ceremonies of the Church of Rome. Jeanne Cauvin probably died early in about 1515. Gérard was devoted to his children, but his desire to get on in the world, and help them to get on, over-ruled everything else. His shrewd eye noted the talents of John, and he sought to give him the finest education he could provide, but it is likely that the sensitive soul of the boy yearned for more of his father's affection.

In the providence of God, while still a child, John came to the notice of the Bishop of Noyon, a member of one of the leading families of the region, the Montmors. He became a member of the household of the bishop's brother, Adrien, where he was treated with great kindness. He was educated (at his father's expense) along with the Montmor sons, Joachim, Yves and a third whose name is unknown to history, but who later took refuge in Geneva in 1547.

Sharing the same tutor were the cousins of these brothers, Claude, abbot of Saint-Eloi, one of the two abbeys of Noyon, and Jean, canon of Evreux, who later became Bishop and Count of Noyon in 1532. It was to Claude that John afterwards dedicated his first book, a commentary on Seneca's *De Clementia*, acknowledging with gratitude the debt he owed to this most noble family:

> I owe you all that I am and have . . . As a boy I was brought up in your home and was initiated in my studies with you. Hence I owe to your noble family my first training in life and letters.

These are the words of the grandson of a one-time boatman-cooper, 'merely a man from among the common people', as he once described himself. Yet, through his connections with the Montmors, John Calvin became, in the words of one of his biographers, 'polished, self-assured, and independent'—a figure who would not be out of his depth among the company of the great families of France.

While John was still a boy of twelve, his father secured an ecclesiastical appointment for him from which he derived an income. It was no strange thing in those days that someone so young should be made a clerk and receive the tonsure; Pope Benedictus IX received the papal crown at that tender age, and it was not uncommon for boys of eight, ten, or twelve to be made cardinals. They reaped the bulk of the income from the office and paid for someone else to do the duties for a small sum. The traffic in church appointments was one of the evils of the age. 'The house of God was made a house of merchandise', says one of Calvin's biographers. 'The Pope and money ruled there, but for Christ there was no place.'

John was a quiet and retiring child, delicate and pale, timorous, yet also passionate. Into his pale cheeks, it was said, colour and glow came as he sat poring over his books. Perhaps in 1520 or 1521, when he was eleven or twelve years old, he went up to Paris with the Montmors to further his studies. At the Collège de la Marche he undertook a course of preparation that would fit him for the study of philosophy in the Faculty of Arts at the university. This

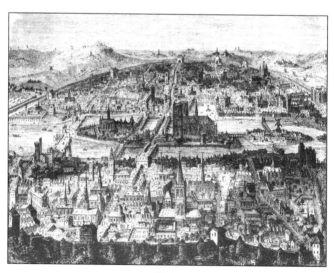

Paris.

preliminary course would have included Latin grammar, poetry, a secretarial training in the writing of letters to persons of varying ranks, as well as a certain amount of arithmetic.

It was here that the young Calvin sat under one of the great Latin scholars of the age, Mathurin Cordier. To him John was to dedicate his Commentary on 1 Thessalonians, acknowledging the debt he owed him for the training he had received. He later brought his old teacher to Geneva to be master of the city's grammar school. Cordier was to survive Calvin by a few months, dying at a good old age.

After a year or so, Calvin was adjudged to have made sufficient progress to enter the University's Arts degree course, and so he transferred to the Collège de Montaigu. Student

Collège de Montaigu.

life in this college was hard and the discipline rigorous. The day began at four in the morning and was filled with lectures, discussions, readings, prayers and other religious exercises, before ending at eight or nine in the evening. One of the religious exercises encouraged was the denunciation of one another that took place at a weekly examination of behaviour. Perhaps this practice was the basis for the much-quoted statement that Calvin was nicknamed 'the accusative case' because of his deep seriousness and strict sobriety.

Be that as it may, what is abundantly clear is that Calvin was 'a friendly, attractive, lovable youth' of irreproachable life and frank manners. Wherever he went he inspired affection in others.

In the 1520s another student entered the gates of the French capital, a dark Spaniard—Ignatius Loyola. We do not know if the two ever met. One, a young teenager, was to become the great leader of the Protestant Reformation, while the other, a man of thirty-six, was to become, as founder of the Jesuit order, a driving force behind the defence of papal authority.

In 1525 or 1526 Calvin obtained his Master of Arts degree. His father had intended him for a career in the Church and so a degree in theology would have been the next step on the way to the priesthood. But at this time, perhaps with the disruptive influences of the Reformation movement looming ever larger in the background, Gérard now considered that a career in law offered better financial prospects for his promising son than a career in the Church. Many years later, in his Preface to his Commentary on the Psalms Calvin tells of his father's change of mind:

When I was as yet a very little boy, my father had destined me for the study of theology. But afterwards, when he considered that the legal profession commonly raised those who followed it to wealth, this prospect induced him suddenly to change his purpose. Thus it came to pass, that I was withdrawn from the study of philosophy, and was put to the study of law.

Between 1525/26 and 1531 Calvin studied law at the universities of Orléans and Bourges, sitting at the feet of two great teachers: Pierre de l'Estoile and the famous Italian jurist Andreas Alciati. As a dutiful son Calvin worked hard and excelled in his studies. It is said of him that after a day at classes he would return to his lodgings, take a light supper, and sit up till midnight reading his books. Then in the morning he would wake early and review in his mind what he had studied the evening before. Thus his mind became well stored, but the long hours left their mark on his constitution. Theodore Beza noted:

> By these continual vigils he attained his substantial learning and pre-eminent memory, but it is also likely that he brought on that weakness of stomach that was the cause of his various illnesses and at length of his early death.

During his student days at Paris, Orléans and Bourges Calvin made a number of important friendships that were to have a significant bearing upon his life. Among these friends were two men who had already taken steps towards the ranks of the Reformation. The first was Pierre Robert, a relative of Calvin and a brilliant young man, who has been called the Henry Martyn of the French Reformation. One practice he shared with his cousin—working late into

the night—gave rise to his nick-
name Olivetanus or Midnight
Oil. The joke stuck and became
his surname. He was probably
at Paris with Calvin. In 1528, to
escape persecution in Orléans,
Olivétan fled to the Reformed
city of Strasbourg. Beza believed
he was responsible for Calvin's
conversion: 'When he had been
taught about true religion by a
certain kinsman, Pierre Robert

Melchior Wolmar (1497-1561).

Olivétan, he began to devote himself to reading the Bible, to
abhor superstitions, and so to separate himself from those
rites.' The other friend was Melchior Wolmar, thirteen years
Calvin's senior. Their paths crossed in the Faculty of Arts
in Paris. Wolmar was a gifted linguist who devoted himself
to the study of Greek. It was probably towards the end of
their time in Orléans that he began to teach Greek to Calvin,
but even before then a life-long friendship between the two
men had begun. According to some writers, it was Wolmar
who won Calvin for the evangelical faith.

In 1531 Gérard Cauvin died. After completing his legal
studies at Orléans and Bourges, Calvin returned to Paris and
attached himself to the Collège Fortet, where he continued
his study of Greek and began learning Hebrew. In his Preface to his *Commentary on the Psalms*, Calvin tells of his
conversion which turned him from the law to the gospel:

> Since I was too obstinately devoted to the superstition
> of Popery to be easily extricated from so profound an

abyss of mire, God by a sudden conversion subdued and brought my mind to a teachable frame.[1]

He evidently passed through deep conviction of sin, and saw himself in danger of eternal death before he looked to God for eternal life. In a letter of later date to Cardinal Sadoleto,[2] he defended himself against charges of heresy and schism, and said that when he was still in the Roman Church he found that the leaders of that Church neither understood God's Word nor greatly cared for it: 'They only drove the unhappy people to and fro with strange doctrines and deluded them with I know not what strange follies. Every place was filled with pernicious errors, falsehoods, and superstitions.' He told the cardinal that when he had performed all the works the Church demanded (confession, good works, sacrifices, etc.), he was still far off from true peace. Appealing to God, he could say:

> Whenever I descended into myself or raised my head to Thee, terror seized me—terror which no expiations or satisfactions could cure. And the more closely I examined myself the sharper were the stings with which my conscience was pricked.

So it was that Calvin came to repentance and faith, submitting himself with his whole heart to the righteousness of God in Christ. God had shone upon him with the brightness of his Spirit and had made clear to him there was no light which could direct his soul into the way of life other than

---

[1] *Commentary on the Book of Psalms*, vol. 1 (Edinburgh: Calvin Translation Society, 1845), p. xl.

[2] This letter, along with very many others, is to be found in John Calvin, *Tracts and Letters*, 7 vols. (Edinburgh: Banner of Truth, 2009).

that which is in his Word. He now saw that there was one sacrifice alone which satisfied divine justice and reconciled us to God, and that those who put confidence in their own good works were ignorant as to what 'good works' really were in the sight of God. He came to faith and peace in much the same way as did Martin Luther.

The date of Calvin's conversion is not known and has been the subject of much conjecture among historians. It had been customary to place it in 1532 or even 1533. But Emile Doumergue argued strongly that, while the change was complete in 1532, it had commenced some years earlier. Recent writers tend to agree with this and think that his conversion took place sometime in 1529 or 1530, during his days at the University of Bourges.

The hand of Providence was manifest in the ordering of Calvin's ways. How rich was his preparation for his future life's work! The best Latin scholar of his generation, Mathurin Cordier, taught him in Paris and the gifted Melchior Wolmar taught him Greek at Orléans and Bourges. But they both spoke to him also of the gospel of Christ. It was his privilege to be instructed by the most illustrious professors of law of that time—l'Estoile and Alciati—and they 'moulded his mind to that kind of precise, exact, realistic thinking which permits him to be not

Andreas Alciatus (1482-1550).

merely the theologian but the legislator of the Reformation'. His early life and student days in Paris had shown him the failings and vices of the Roman Church.

And 'by the side of the shadow designed to repel him shines the light destined to attract him', for he became the friend of the early French lovers of the truth, some of whom were to seal their testimony with their blood. He was even to meet in Paris with Servetus, the anti-Trinitarian who was to shock him with his dangerous heresies. Thus, in his all-controlling providence and in such various ways, God fashioned the youthful David to meet the towering Goliaths of the age.

Part of the first chapter of Genesis from Olivétan's French Bible.

The Cathedral of Nôtre Dame, Paris.

TWO

WANDERINGS AND FLIGHT

IN HIS PREFACE to his Commentary on the Psalms
Calvin tells us this of the period following his 'sudden
conversion':

> Having thus received some taste and knowledge of true
> godliness, I was immediately inflamed with so intense a
> desire to make progress therein, that although I did not
> altogether leave off other studies, I yet pursued them with
> less ardour. I was quite surprised to find that before a year
> had elapsed, all who had any desire after purer doctrine
> were continually coming to me to learn, although I myself
> was as yet but a mere novice and a tyro.

It might be supposed that his precise words, 'before a year
had elapsed', would make it possible to pin-point the date
of his conversion. But, as already noted, the date cannot be
determined with any certainty. It has been suggested that
the traditional translation of *subita* as 'sudden' may be mis-
leading, for Calvin himself is known, in a different context,
to have understood the Latin to mean 'unexpected'. There
are other indications that his conversion may have been
more a process than a sudden event. His later testimony to

Cardinal Sadoleto would bear that interpretation: 'Offended by the novelty, I lent an unwilling ear, and at first, I confess, strenuously and passionately resisted.' Traditions record that before he left the study of law at Bourges, in 1530 or 1531, he was preaching in that region. In Asnières, 'his word sowed seeds that have never been stifled'. In Linières he preached in an old barn by the river, where one of his hearers reported, 'He tells us something new.'

On leaving Bourges, Calvin was chiefly in Paris, at the Collège Fortet, as mentioned in the last chapter. In April 1532 he had printed his first book, at his own expense, a Commentary on Seneca's *Treatise on Clemency*. He was then twenty-two. Some have concluded from the humanist, non-religious standpoint of this work that Calvin had not yet known conversion. That judgment would appear to be a mistake. Nevertheless Calvin intended the work to be a learned essay designed to demonstrate his scholarship. When Calvin prepared the work he was not yet the evangelist he would become, and no doubt the statement, 'All who had any desire after purer doctrine were continually coming to me to learn', refers to the circle of friends that began to group round him once he settled in Paris. A frequent meeting place was probably the house of Étienne de la Forge, a noble merchant who was soon to suffer martyrdom. Tradition has it that Calvin generally closed his exhortations to his friends with the words: 'If God be for us, who can be against us?'

Evangelical belief was not, however, to remain spoken only in private homes. On the morning of All Saints' Day, 1 November 1533, Paris was startled. On that day Calvin's friend, Nicholas Cop, who had been appointed rector of the

University, was to deliver an inaugural address. He asked Calvin to prepare it for him and Calvin consented. The text was Matthew 5:3, 'Blessed are the poor in spirit.' The address was a plea for the reformation of the Church on the basis of a pure gospel. It was a bold venture, for only recently Protestant 'heretics' had been committed to the flames in Paris. Yet now a manifesto of Protestantism was issued in its very citadel of learning. The University authorities were enraged. A price was put on Cop's head and the prisons were filled with 'Lutherans' destined to the stake. Cop took refuge in flight. Calvin too fell under suspicion. The story that he escaped out of his window by making a rope of his bed-sheets rests on the authority of one of his early biographers, Papire Masson. Beza's simpler version is more worthy of credence—Calvin was fortunately not in his room when they came to take him. A police officer named Morin who was noted for his harshness and brutality raided the Collège Fortet and seized his books, papers and letters. We regret the loss of those letters—they might have filled some gaps in our knowledge of Calvin in those early days.

Queen Margaret of Navarre, the king's sister, was well disposed to the Protestants and hastened to use her influence to stop the persecution. She was in friendly relations with Calvin and esteemed him highly. He had evidently not gone far from the capital, and after Queen Margaret's intervention he returned. Beza tells us that on his return he was 'most honourably received' by Queen Margaret. But his stay was brief. The atmosphere was too hot in the capital. He betook himself at the end of 1533 or beginning of 1534 to the safer air of Angoulême, in the south-west of France. There he found refuge with Louis du Tillet, canon of the cathedral, whom he had known at the University. He went by an assumed name, Charles d'Espeville. His host showed him kindness, Calvin tells us, 'for the sake of letters'. Du Tillet prized the learning of his friend. Calvin speaks mournfully of his 'idleness' at Angoulême. But he could not be idle. He was so assiduous at his work, says one of his biographers, that he spent whole nights without sleep and days without food. He wrote sermons and brief exhortations at the request of du Tillet. The statements of faith which he drew up here for the instruction of new converts were afterwards, we believe, to form the basis of his great work the *Institutes of the Christian Religion*. Far from being idle, 'Angoulême was the forge of the new Vulcan'. In

Lefèvre d'Etaples (1455-1536).

his discussions with du Tillet and a few other friends he would sometimes say, 'Let us find the truth.' The truth was not merely to be sought; it was possible to find it! After this visit to Angoulême, he went farther south to Nérac to see Lefèvre d'Etaples, a distinguished scholar and early advocate of evangelical reform, who was sheltering there under the protection of the Queen of Navarre. The old man met the youth with delight and prophesied of him that he would be an instrument in restoring the kingdom of God in France. When the Queen of Navarre about this time showed favour to some mystics whose teaching Calvin esteemed dangerous, he refuted their errors. The Queen was displeased. In defence he said: 'A dog barks if he sees someone attacking his master; I would be very cowardly if I saw the truth of God assailed and remained silent.'

The Queen of Navarre.

In May 1534, Calvin went to Noyon to resign his clerical appointments. He was now twenty-five years old and so had reached the age when, according to the law of the Church, he must either enter into 'holy orders' or resign his benefices. He took the latter course. This step was determined by his age and was the result of convictions formed years before. At Noyon, according to a colourful but inaccurate account, he was put in prison for 'a tumult made in a church', was released then rearrested. The story is based on a case of mistaken identity.[1]

He made a brief visit to Paris, and then returned to Angoulême, but not to stay. He had decided to leave France that he might live 'more peaceably and according to his

---

[1] Older writers believed that Calvin fell foul of the authorities in Noyon during this visit in May 1534. They accepted Abel Lefranc's misreading of a registry entry for 26 May which recorded that a John Calvin 'was put in prison at the gate Corbaut, for an uproar made in church on the eve of Trinity Sunday'. However, the facts are less dramatic if no less interesting: Calvin had a namesake (*Un Iean Cauvin, dict Mudit* . . . 'A Jean Cauvin, called Mudit . . .' following the correct reading of the register). T. H. L. Parker humorously adds: 'This namesake was presumably the same who in 1551–2 (when our Jean Cauvin had a water-tight alibi, being in Geneva at the time) was evicted from his canonry for having kept in his house "*une femme de mauvaise gouvernement*"'!

conscience'. He and du Tillet set out together and first of all proceeded north to Poitiers. Here he met with a select group of friends in private conferences and meetings for worship. He prayed that the Spirit would descend on the little flock which gathered to hear his expositions of the Scriptures. He celebrated the Lord's Supper with apostolic simplicity, divesting it of the popish ceremonies which had gathered round it. On one occasion Charles de Sage disputed with him about 'the sacrifice of the mass'. Calvin had his Bible before him and indicating it he exclaimed: 'That is my Mass!' Then he bared his head, throwing his cap on the table, and lifted his eyes to heaven with the cry: 'Lord, if on the day of judgment you rebuke me because I have not been at Mass, but have forsaken it, I shall answer, "Lord, you have not commanded it. Here is your law. Here is the Scripture which is the rule you have given me, and in it I find no other sacrifice than that which is offered on the cross."' For safety the little group met in a cave outside the city. His host at Poitiers advised him to go; his presence had become known to the authorities. So he went north-east to Orléans, which is within easy reach of Paris.

Here, in 1534, he wrote his first religious publication. It was entitled *Psychopannychia*. In the preface he tells us that he had been urged for some time to this task by some good people of note. In this book he corrects the notions of certain Anabaptists with whom Calvin was in contact, and who maintained that the souls of the departed sleep till the last judgment. It is evident that this youth of twenty-five was now esteemed a leader of the church.

With du Tillet he went away westward to Strasbourg. Near Metz they fell into an awkward plight through the villainy of one of their two servants who made off with one of their horses and all their money. Fortunately the other servant had ten crowns in his pocket which sufficed till they reached Strasbourg.

From Strasbourg they went without delay to Basel, which was a self-governing city where sympathy for the Reformation was strong. In this city he would no doubt be re-united with his friend, Nicholas Cop, whom he had not seen since the famous episode in Paris on All Saints' Day, 1533. He lodged with an honourable matron, Catherine Klein. Over thirty years later the venerable lady still spoke of him often and with enthusiasm—she was still under the marvellous spell of the godly and gifted Reformer. 'Here', she would say, 'he wrote and elaborated in the watches of the night the *Institutes of the Christian Religion*.' Those night-watches were 'memorable and heavenly'. They were to mean more than tongue could tell to countless thousands then and since. It was no mere academic task to which this author set himself. The *Institutes* was written in defence of his brothers in France who were being burnt as heretics and slandered as revolutionaries. They were no heretics and no revolutionaries. Here was the manifesto and confession of their faith—addressed to no less a personage than the king of France himself—in words that were eloquent and argument that was incomparable. What was begun at Angoulême in 1534 was fashioned at Basel in 1535 to meet a crying need.

CHRISTIA

NAE RELIGIONIS INSTI-
tutio, totam ferè pietatis summā, & quic
quid est in doctrina salutis cognitu ne-
cessarium, complectens : omnibus pietatis studiosis lectu dignissi-
mum opus, ac re
cens edi-
tum.

PRAEFATIO AD CHRI
stianißimum REGEM FRANCIAE, *qua
hic ei liber pro confeßione fidei
offertur.*

IOANNE CALVINO
Nouiodunensi autore.

BASILEAE,
M. D. XXXVI.

Title page of the first edition of Calvin's *Institutes of the Christian Religion,*
published in Basel, 1536.

THREE

A PROTESTANT MANIFESTO

IT WAS IN 1534 that Calvin determined to leave his native France. In February 1535 he came to the free city of Basel. So it came to pass that in this city his *Institutes of the Christian Religion* was first printed.

Francis I, king of France, had wavered between a policy of clemency toward the Protestants and one of severity. Now a daring deed on the part of some of the boldest of the Protestants hastened him to align himself with their persecutors.

Francis I.

Placards or posters attacking the Mass were affixed to public buildings in many of the chief towns of France on the night of 17 October 1534. They bore this title: 'Truthful Articles concerning the horrible, great and unbearable abuses of the popish Mass, invented directly against the Holy Supper of our Lord, the only Mediator and Saviour, Jesus Christ.' Then followed an attack on the Pope, the cardinals, the bishops, and the monks. The man behind the placards was long thought to be William Farel; actually they were drawn up by Antoine Marcourt, the leading pastor of Neuchâtel. One placard was even fixed to the door of the king's own bedroom. When the people of Paris awoke and read the placards, they felt as if they had been struck by a thunder-bolt! Their sense of outrage led to an outburst of fanaticism in defence of the Catholic Faith.

The king's own rage knew no bounds. Two hundred Protestants were cast into prison. Some had their hands cut off; others had their tongues torn out. The shoemaker, Milon, lame and paralysed, was the first to the stake. By the November 10, seven had been condemned to death, and during the next three months several more were to share their fate (including Calvin's friend, Etienne de la Forge); some were executed in the king's own presence.

The Protestants now fled like a flock of sheep pursued by fierce wolves. Some of the fugitives reached Basel. Terrible were the tidings they brought. It was not only the barbarous cruelty of Francis to his beloved brethren which roused Calvin; it was the king's slanderous falsehood.

Francis had amused himself over the charred bodies of his Protestant subjects, but he did not want to lose the support of the Protestant princes of Germany in his struggle with the Emperor, Charles V. So Francis wrote to them on 1 February 1535, stating that the persecuted French Protestants were dangerous revolutionaries; they were like a contagious and devastating plague, he alleged. To get over the difficulty of proof, he said, 'I have preferred to bury their particular theses in the darkness from which they sprang rather than send them to you who are the light of the world.' This was a subtle ploy on Francis' part, for since the Peasants' War of 1524–25 and the extravagances of some of the Anabaptists, the German Protestant princes abhorred the very thought of revolutionary ideas.

Charles V.

But God had his man ready for the vindication of his persecuted saints. Calvin, as we have seen, in the previous chapter, had been at work at Angoulême in 1534 preparing doctrinal statements for the instruction of the children of God. Now he hurried on with the work he had started and published it in March 1536. The *Institutes of the Christian Religion* was the first book he published after he devoted himself to the service of God.

Many years later, in his Preface to his Commentary on the Psalms (1557), Calvin speaks of his one great object: to live in seclusion without being known so that he might make more progress in the knowledge of true godliness. He left France expressly for the purpose of enjoying in some obscure corner the repose which he had always desired but had been so long denied.

> But lo! while I lay hidden at Basel, and known only to a few people, many faithful and holy persons were burnt alive in France; and report of these burnings having reached foreign nations, they excited the strongest

disapprobation among a great part of the Germans, whose indignation was kindled against the authors of such tyranny. In order to allay this indignation, certain wicked and lying pamphlets were circulated, stating, that none were treated with such cruelty but Anabaptists and seditious persons, who, by their perverse railings and false opinions, were overthrowing not only religion but also all civil order.

Not only did such lies seek to cover the guilt of the innocent blood already shed; they sought to enable the murderers to proceed to the utmost extremity against the saints in the days ahead and remove all grounds for compassion towards them. So, says Calvin,

> It appeared to me, that unless I opposed them to the utmost of my ability, my silence could not be vindicated from the charge of cowardice and treachery. This was the consideration which induced me to publish my *Institutes of the Christian Religion*. My objects were, first, to prove that these reports were false and calumnious, and thus to vindicate my brethren, whose death was precious in the sight of the Lord; and next, that as the same cruelties might very soon after be exercised against many unhappy individuals, foreign nations might be touched with at least some compassion toward them and solicitude about them.

Calvin, his heart filled with pity for his suffering brethren, and indignation over the conduct of the king, penned a Dedication to his book and addressed it to Francis himself. Its pages are among the most celebrated ever written by the Reformer:

When I began this work, Sire, nothing was further from my thoughts than writing a book which would afterwards be presented to your Majesty. My intention was only to lay down some elementary principles, by which inquirers on the subject of religion might be instructed in the nature of true piety. And this labour I undertook chiefly for my own countrymen, the French, of whom I apprehended multitudes to be hungering and thirsting after Christ, but saw very few possessing any real knowledge of him. That this was my design, the book itself proves by its simple method and unadorned composition. But when I perceived that the fury of certain wicked men in your kingdom had grown to such a height as to leave no room in the land for sound doctrine, I thought I should be usefully employed if in the same work I delivered my instructions to them and exhibited my confession to you, that you may know the nature of that doctrine, which is the object of such unbounded rage to those madmen who are now disturbing the country with fire and sword.

He enumerates the calumnies which were being heaped on the persecuted, and brings the Dedication to a conclusion with these noble words:

If your Majesty's ears are so pre-occupied with the whispers of the malevolent as to leave no opportunity for the accused to speak for themselves, and if these outrageous furies with your connivance continue to persecute with imprisonments, scourges, tortures, confiscations and flames, we shall indeed, like sheep destined to the slaughter, be reduced to great extremities. Yet shall we in patience possess our souls, and wait for the mighty hand of the Lord, which undoubtedly will in time appear, and show itself armed for the deliverance of the poor from their affliction, and for the punishment of their despisers, who now exult in such perfect security. May the Lord, the King of kings, establish your throne with righteousness and your kingdom with equity.

Emile Doumergue comments on the Dedication: 'Francis I and Calvin! The one after long hesitation had just put himself at the head of the persecutors, and the other after long preparation had just put himself at the head of the persecuted . . . The king who is truly king is not Francis I; it is Calvin.'

The 1536 edition of the *Institutes* differs little in subject matter from the author's final edition of 1559. But it was much smaller. Calvin calls it a 'brief handbook' and 'a little booklet', though it was no insignificant volume. Many revisions passed through his hands and while the same truth is presented in the final edition, the arrangement is altered and the book has grown to five times its original size. On the final edition he laboured the more, knowing himself to be a dying man.

The first edition of the *Institutes* was in Latin, as Doumergue has clearly shown – not in French, as some writers have asserted. It was written for men of all nations, Latin being everywhere understood by men of education.

When Calvin published his first book back in April 1532 (his commentary on Seneca's treatise, *On Clemency*), he was 'quivering with anxiety' that it might be successful. Less than four years had passed since then, and it is a token of the revolution wrought within him that when he now issued his *Institutes* he was free from all such concerns. Living at Basel under the pseudonym 'Lucanius' he was content that none should know him to be the author. Immediately after issuing it – probably even before it came from the press – he left Basel for Italy, not waiting to see how it would fare.

Says Warfield:

> In the immense upheavals of the Reformation movement the foundations of faith seemed to many to be broken up, and the most important questions to be set adrift; extravagances of all sorts sprang up on every side . . . It was Calvin's *Institutes* which, with its calm, clear, positive exposition of the evangelical faith on the irrefragable authority of the Holy Scriptures, gave stability to wavering minds, and confidence to sinking hearts, and placed upon the lips of all a brilliant apology, in the face of the calumnies of the enemies of the Reformation.

And this was the work of a young man of just twenty-six years of age!

The Castle at Ferrara, Italy.

FOUR

ARRIVAL IN GENEVA

A T THE END of Calvin's Preface to the *Institutes* there was the date '23 August 1535' and at the end of the volume the date of its publication 'March 1536'. It was probably in February 1536—before the first edition of his *Institutes* appeared—that Calvin left Basel for Italy in the company of his friend, Louis du Tillet. 'Italy must be visited'—so said du Tillet; but the visit turned out to be a brief one. Calvin said that he entered Italy only to leave it. The travellers journeyed under assumed names. Ferrara was their destination. It lies in the Po valley, not far from Venice. The Duchess of Ferrara, a daughter of Louis XII of France, had an open ear for the gospel. Calvin, Beza tells us, 'confirmed her in her zeal for true religion'. She held him in the highest esteem, and a correspondence was kept up between them. While he was spared, she had a counsellor firm, fearless, and wise.

We are not to think of him as preaching openly in Ferrara, but rather discreetly witnessing amid a circle of friends. It was necessary to proceed warily, as the Duke did not share the views of his wife. Indeed, the Duchess was to suffer for her faith and for her friendship with the 'heretics'. Calvin spent at most only a few months in Ferrara. His departure was, no doubt, hastened by an event which took place on Good Friday, 14 April 1536. A young singer by the name Jehannet, who was employed in the service of the Duchess, ostentatiously walked out of the church

Renée, Duchess of Ferrara
(1510-74).

service in protest against the adoration of the cross. He was seized and under torture admitted not only that he was a 'heretic', but that most of those at the court were likewise. Within a short time many of them sought safer quarters elsewhere—among them Calvin.

We find the Reformer again at Paris on 2 June 1536. Apparently he took advantage of the brief respite granted to the French Protestants at that time by the recently issued Edict of Lyon. Not long after, though, he was on the move again, leaving Paris with the intention of settling in the Protestant city of Strasbourg, 'safe from the storms and the prelate's rage'. He probably made a short stay at Lyon en route. Due to circumstances beyond his control he was forced to take a detour, which was to include a brief stop-over in the city of Geneva in August 1536. Here his plans were to be completely altered. Calvin had resolved to continue in 'privacy and obscurity'. But he says, 'William Farel detained me at Geneva, not so much by counsel and exhortation, as by a dreadful imprecation.'

A few years earlier, in the autumn of 1532, Farel had come to Geneva, and by his exertions and those of Peter Viret popery had been driven from the city. Farel and Viret were remarkable men—full of zeal and energy. Farel had on occasion been beaten by the Romanists till he was a mass of wounds and blood. Viret bore a wound on his shoulder received from the sword of a priest in an ambush. Having failed to kill him with the sword, his enemies sought to poison him and almost succeeded—leaving his health permanently undermined.

It was only a few brief months before Calvin's arrival that the Reformation had been officially accepted in Geneva—on 25 May 1536. As Calvin was later to record, 'Matters were not yet brought to a settled state, and the city was divided into unholy and dangerous factions.' Again many years later he could say, 'When I came to this church, it had practically nothing. There was preaching and that was all. The idols were sought out and burned, and there was no other reformation. All was in confusion.' The work was too much for Farel, even with all his tremendous energy. To his great credit he recognized the need for someone with the ability to teach and to bring order to the church, and his quick eye evidently detected such gifts in the twenty-seven-year-old Calvin.

Just one night in Geneva, then on to Strasbourg—that was Calvin's intention. But his old friend du Tillet, who was now living in Geneva (and who later apostatized and returned to the Roman Church!), discovered his friend's presence in the city and made it known to the other brethren. There then followed the famous scene often depicted. Farel hastened to the inn where Calvin was staying and set before the visitor the pressing spiritual needs of Geneva and begged him to stay. Calvin replied that his heart was set on devoting himself to his private studies. The more Farel urged, the more Calvin was dismayed at the prospect so suddenly opening up before him. Then the older man, 'quivering with a holy passion', started up and cried with his voice of thunder: 'I declare this to you in the name of God Almighty. You give your studies as an excuse, but if you refuse to devote yourself here with us to this work of the Lord, God will curse you, for you seek your own interests rather than Christ's.' Calvin confesses that he was so 'stricken with terror' by this frightful imprecation that he desisted from his onward journey.

It was as if God had stretched forth his hand from on high to stop him. Calvin had been forced to make the detour to Geneva because of troop movements which effectively barred the direct road to Strasbourg. Moreover, Farel had been absent from Geneva for over a month, and the City Council had to write to him on 10 July to urge him to return, as certain matters required his presence. If Farel had delayed his return to Geneva by just a few days, Calvin would have been on his way and gone for good. But the arrangements of Providence are exact! 'A man's heart plans his way: but the LORD directs his steps' (*Prov.* 16:9).

Calvin heard the divine call, bowed his head and obeyed. First of all, he went to Basel to put his affairs in order. On his return to Geneva, he fell ill with a heavy cold which lingered on through the autumn—illness was destined to seize upon a frame already weakened by the rigours of study and would make his life of unremitting toil an outstanding example of patient endurance. At the beginning of September 1536, he lectured in St Peter's on the Epistles of St Paul. His addresses were received with great 'commendation and profit'. On 5 September Farel set forth before the Council the need for this ministry of Calvin and the councillors' duty of making provision for its support. The Council were clearly not as enamoured with the new preacher as was Farel—they did not even enter his name in the records, but rather disparagingly referred to him as 'that Frenchman'. It was nearly five months before Calvin received any remuneration for his services in the city. His coming was a great event in the purposes of God; but it passed almost without notice by men!

William Farel (1489-1565).

Calvin threatened while preaching in Geneva.

FIVE

FIRST MINISTRY IN GENEVA

IN THE EARLY DAYS of the Reformation in Switzerland public debates served the cause well. Shortly after Calvin came to Geneva, it was arranged—on the initiative of the city of Berne—to hold a public debate in the cathedral at Lausanne from 1 to 8 October 1536. Farel and Viret were to be the disputants on the one side, with representatives of the Roman Church on the other. The debate opened on Sunday, 1 October, with a sermon by Farel, and it closed with another sermon from him the following Sunday. Farel had drawn up ten theses. He took the lead in defending the first, on justification by faith. Viret took the lead in defending the third, against the 'bodily presence' in the Lord's Supper. Around these points the main debate revolved. From seven o'clock on the Monday morning the crowd filled the huge cathedral. Of 337 priests invited, only 174 were present, and of these only four took part in the debate, as they defended the dogmas of the Papacy.

Farel underscored the difference between Protestant liberty and Roman intolerance when he cried:

You are free to speak boldly. We carry on the contest here not with faggot or fire or sword or prison or torture. The executioners are not here as teachers or as powerful arguments, but the truth of Scripture . . . The truth is strong enough against the lie; if you have it, present it.

Where could one find such an offer where Romanism prevails?

Thursday, 5 October came. Calvin had not yet intervened. Indeed, he had resolved to say nothing; he was satisfied with the answers of Farel and Viret. The debate was on the 'real presence' of Christ in the Supper. A Romanist read a long and carefully prepared paper. He accused the Protestants of ignoring the Fathers. Calvin then rose to his feet. From memory he cited several Church Fathers; he quoted from Tertullian, a sermon attributed to Chrysostom, and some passages from Augustine. His acquaintance with the Fathers was unequalled, his irony devastating. His adversaries were overwhelmed and silent. Amid tense excitement a monk, Jean Tandi, who had been present from the beginning, arose and told the whole assembly that he was convinced of the truth of the Reformers' doctrine—convinced that it accorded with the Scriptures. He asked pardon from God and from the people and declared that from now on he would renounce the garb of his order and live as a Christian.

Farel immediately cried, 'O how great and good and wise God is! He has had pity on the poor sheep wandering in the wilderness, and has led him to his holy fold.' The gathering broke up. Other Romanists avowed their new-found faith. One priest cried, 'I know I will be excommunicated, but yet I come to find the truth.' In the three months which followed, more than 80 monks and 120 priests and curates came over to the Protestant cause.

The next day the Council of Lausanne introduced measures to clear the city of vice, and a few weeks later the city of Berne ordered the removal of all images and altars, the abolition of popish ceremonies and the 'sacrifice of the Mass'.

So Calvin came to be the acknowledged and respected leader of the Reformed movement. At the great Swiss synod meeting in Berne from 16–18 October 1536, at which 296 churches were represented, the Lutheran Formula of Concord was debated. The Strasbourg Reformers Bucer and Capito recommended it, but the Swiss churches for the most part were not in favour of it. However, one Swiss pastor arose to plead for unity among the various national churches. Emile Doumergue believes this pastor was John Calvin, and his assumption may well be correct.

Calvin's first ministry at Geneva turned out to be brief— just a year and eight months. Yet he accomplished much amid many difficulties. Among his achievements were the Articles on the Organization of the Church and its Worship at Geneva—adopted by the Council on 16 January 1537. Much of the church order and discipline in Geneva, against which Calvin's critics sometimes rage, was already in existence before his arrival, due to the work of Farel. At Zurich, too, church discipline was already operating. But Calvin supplemented Farel's arrangements, and in the Articles of 1537 he insisted on the church's right to excommunicate offenders. He also introduced the singing of Psalms and certain Canticles. The two Reformers, moreover, expressed their opinion that it was desirable to celebrate the Lord's Supper every Lord's day. However, all they asked for in the current circumstances was that it be celebrated once a month; nevertheless, the Council fixed upon its observance four times a year.

In the winter of 1536–37 Calvin drew up his first Catechism for the instruction of the young. The title of the edition, which was issued early in 1537, was the *Instruction Used in the Church of Geneva*. In later years he revised this document carefully and altered its substance and arrangement. This Catechism was his first work in the French language; a Latin edition followed it to the press early in 1538. It was 'a short and easy summary of the faith' and dealt with the Apostles' Creed, the Ten Commandments and the Lord's Prayer.

The Catechism was followed by another important document, of 42 pages, the *Confession of Faith*. All the citizens were required to subscribe to it in order 'to recognize those in harmony with the gospel and those preferring to be of the kingdom of the pope than of the kingdom of Christ'. The Confession was the joint work of Calvin and Farel.

Only a few months after he came to Geneva, Calvin was troubled by the arrival of certain opponents. One was the poor, half-crazy fanatic and anti-Trinitarian, Claude Aliodi. Then two Anabaptists appeared. Doumergue describes the Anabaptists as 'these most dangerous enemies of the Reformation in its early days, these Protestants who

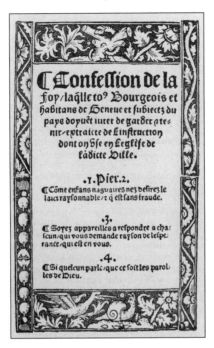

The title page of the Confession of
Faith of Geneva, 1537.

gave cause for so many charges and slanders against the
Protestants'. In the public disputation which ensued Calvin
'so thoroughly refuted them by the Word of God alone, on
18 March 1537, that from that time not more than one or
two appeared in that Church' (Theodore Beza).

Within the city there was increasing opposition to
the programme of reform. A large number of citizens
refused to sign the Confession. Many objected to the

strictness of the rule barring from the Lord's table those who were loose in their lives. A politically-strong party which suspected the loyalty of Calvin and Farel (who were, of course, both French) began to intercept their letters and spy upon them continually. We can perhaps feel something of the difficulties facing the Reformers from a letter written to Calvin in March 1538 by two Englishmen, who had spent four months in Geneva. The English visitors not only expressed their admiration of his gentleness and pleasantness of character and the charm of his conversation, but their regret at the trouble which evil men were causing him.

While the opposition at Geneva was increasing, Calvin was plunged into one of the fiercest controversies of his life. At the close of the conference in the cathedral at Lausanne in 1536, Peter Caroli succeeded in having himself appointed as first pastor of the city, with Viret as his colleague. The noted church historian Philip Schaff described Caroli as 'an unprincipled, vain and quarrelsome theological adventurer and turncoat'. This strong language is abundantly justified. In a sermon at Lausanne during Viret's absence, Caroli advocated prayers for the dead. Taken to task, he accused Viret and Calvin of Arianism. This touched Calvin to the quick. True, he had not used the words 'Person' and 'Trinity' in his Geneva Catechism, but he flatly denied that either he or Farel or Viret had any objection to those terms. Challenged by Caroli to sign the ancient Creeds (Apostles', Nicene, and Athanasian), Calvin was impolitic enough to refuse. He would not sign anything on Caroli's orders!

Calvin's one design in this refusal was to make it clear that 'Caroli's insistence that only in the words of these Creeds could faith in the Trinity be expressed' was absurd. Actually, Calvin had used the words 'Person' and 'Trinity' in his *Institutes* of 1536. Moreover, when Caroli was attacking him for not using them in the Catechism of 1537, the Reformer was vigorously engaged in excluding from the Church at Geneva impugners of Trinitarian doctrine! He gave little space to the doctrine in the Catechism because he believed an elaborate explanation was too difficult for babes in Christ.

The synod of Berne heard the case and took action, depriving Caroli of his ministry and issuing certificates of orthodoxy to Calvin, Farel, and Viret. Yet for a time there were widespread suspicions of the Genevan pastors' orthodoxy. Caroli's poison had done its work. All that spring and summer Calvin was busy writing letters here, there, and everywhere, correcting the false reports. Yet, in the whole controversy Calvin's loyalty to his friends Farel and Viret, who were attacked even more than he, was outstanding.

'A succession of dissensions' now arose in Geneva. The Council (since the elections in February 1538 under the influence of the Libertines, the implacable opponents of the Reformers) decreed that the Lord's Supper be denied to none. This cut at the root of Calvin's system of church discipline. On Easter Sunday Calvin and Farel refused to dispense the supper to an unruly people so much at variance among themselves. This led to rioting. The Libertine mob ran through the streets at night, firing guns in uproar outside the Reformers' houses and threatening to throw them into the river with the cry, 'To the Rhône!'

On the Monday the Council deposed Calvin and Farel from their pastoral offices and on the Tuesday ordered that they were to leave the city within three days. They left the same day or the next—23 or 24 April 1538. In the Preface to his Commentary on the Psalms Calvin speaks of his timid disposition and says that these 'violent tempests' were necessary as part of his early training. He adds: 'Although I did not sink under them, yet I was not sustained by such greatness of mind as not to rejoice more than it became me when, in consequence of certain commotions, I was banished from Geneva.' His response to the sentence of banishment was, 'Good! If we had served men, we would have been ill rewarded, but we serve a great Master, who will reward us.' He was free and God's hand was in it.

Martin Bucer (1491-1551)

———

SIX

CALVIN'S MINISTRY IN STRASBOURG

CALVIN WAS DRIVEN OUT of Geneva in April 1538 after a ministry of less than two years. He greeted the sentence of banishment with a sigh of relief after all the emotional agitation and fatigue of the preceding months. It was true that Farel and he were treated with ignominy and that they received an ill reward for their unsparing devotion. But Calvin soon recovered his calm. He realized that God's hand was in it all. Geneva had fallen into the hands of their foes, and those in control in the city would not listen to the Synod of Zurich which, although not uncritical of the Reformers' 'misplaced vigour' and lack of tender heartedness towards 'so undisciplined a people', nevertheless gave their support to the ousted pastors. Indeed, the men of Geneva would not even heed the city of Berne; the leading men of Berne had earlier joined forces, for their own ends, with the enemies of Farel and Calvin in Geneva, but now most of them felt that the Genevese had gone too far in driving the Reformers out!

After quitting Geneva, Calvin and Farel visited Berne and Zurich and eventually arrived in Basel where they found a lodging for a few months (6 June to 18 August 1538) with Johannes Oporinus, the printer of the first edition of Calvin's *Institutes* (1536). Farel and Calvin had reached Basel worn out and drenched with rain; indeed one of the two had almost been carried away in the current of a swollen river they were trying to cross.

Farel left Basel for Neuchâtel on 26 July 1538, but before his departure a letter reached Calvin from Martin Bucer. Bucer was the leading pastor at Strasbourg, and his letter invited Calvin to join him in the ongoing work of Reformation in that city. After Farel's departure a second letter from Bucer arrived, pressing the earlier invitation. Calvin was reluctant to accept, for acceptance meant separation from his beloved Farel. Moreover, he had resolved afresh 'to live in a private station, free from the burden and cares of any public charge'. But, as he says in the Preface to his *Commentary on the Psalms*, 'That most excellent servant of Christ, Martin Bucer, employing a similar kind of remonstrance and protestation as that to which Farel had recourse before [to keep Calvin at Geneva in 1536], drew me back to a new station.'

The gentle Bucer could be as strongly urgent as the thundering Farel: he warned Calvin not to be like Jonah in fleeing from God, lest he too experience the wrath of God. The hand of God was indeed in this. It is one of Calvin's Roman Catholic biographers who tells us that when the Reformer left Strasbourg after his three years ministry there, he was a changed man; his horizon was widened, his knowledge was deepened, and his life was enriched with new experiences.

He preached his first sermon at Strasbourg in September 1538; but here, as at Geneva on his first arrival, he received no salary for several months. He suffered from cold and hunger in the winter of 1538–9 and had to sell many of his books just to keep himself alive. His friend Louis du Tillet, who had tragically returned to the Church of Rome, offered to help but attached such conditions to his offer that Calvin declined it with thanks. 'Did he mean to convert me?' wrote Calvin to Farel. Swiss friends also offered help but he preferred to battle on alone.

Shortly after his arrival at Strasbourg news came of the death of his former colleague and friend, the blind preacher Courauld, who had been expelled from Geneva at the same time as Calvin and Farel. Courauld had found a post as pastor in Orbe, but now he was dead, and it was suspected that he had been murdered. Calvin wrote to Farel, 'I am so bowed down by the death of Corauld that I cannot set a limit to my anguish . . . It is not merely the usual sleeplessness I suffer from . . . My mind is chiefly burdened with that iniquitous deed, which, if my suspicions are well founded, I must bring to light.'

He was troubled too by the arrival in Strasbourg of that miserable wretch, Peter Caroli. On this occasion Calvin, who often displayed such marvellous patience, was carried away by his own vehemence. It was not on Caroli that his lash fell, but on his own friends, Bucer, Matthias Zell and Johannes Sturm. They had drawn up articles of faith without showing them to Calvin and demanded that he sign them to make his position clear in the face of Caroli's insidious attacks. Moreover, they made the demand in such a way that it seemed that if he did not sign, then they would be his adversaries. He had reason to be indignant, but he tells us that on this occasion he passed the bounds of moderation. He said he would sooner die than sign the articles and stormed out of the room.

This scene has furnished some material to Calvin's foes, but let us remember that it is Calvin who describes it to us and exposes his fault. It is Calvin who confesses, 'I have sinned grievously.' And after his outburst his only consolation was in groans and tears: 'This fierce beast, this impatience', he tells his beloved Bucer later, 'is not yet conquered.' A fiery temper? Yes, but mark how on occasion he bore Bucer's frank rebuke with the utmost meekness.

Calvin served as pastor of the French Church at Strasbourg and also as a professor in the Academy made famous by Sturm. He was a great pastor, terrible against the wolves which troubled Christ's flock, but tender toward the doubting, weeping with those that wept. He introduced a sounder discipline in the church; he also brought in a liturgy and taught the people to sing the Psalms. What life and power was in the worship! A young man from Antwerp, a fugitive from persecution, told how he 'wept, not for sadness, but for joy to hear them all singing so heartily, and as they sang giving thanks to God that he had led them to a place where his name is glorified. No one could believe what joy there is in singing the praises and wonders of the Lord in the mother tongue as they are sung here!'

In the mother tongue! And that this might be, Calvin turned poet. He began with Psalms 25 and 46. In 1539 he published a selection of 18 Psalms—eight were compositions of Clement Marot and seven were his own. Emile Doumergue says: 'It was Calvin who guided the choir, translated the first Psalms into verse, chose the melodies, and took the early composers under his wing.'

Amid his labours at Strasbourg, Calvin did not forget the Lord's flock at Geneva. A subtle attack upon Geneva by Cardinal Jacopo Sadoleto drew from Calvin a most powerful reply. The church at Geneva was as dear to him as his own soul. His ministry, which Sadoleto assailed without actually identifying him by name, was received from Christ, and must be defended, if need be, with

Cardinal Jacopo Sadoleto

his blood. Step by step he answered the arguments of the Cardinal and reduced them to ashes. All over Europe men knew that a great champion of the Protestant cause had arisen.

During his sojourn at Strasbourg he commenced writing commentaries on Paul's epistles. His *Commentary on Romans* is dated 18 October 1539. He states the three principles which guided him as an expositor: brevity, simplicity, and liberty of interpretation. At the beginning of August 1540, he married Idelette de Bure, the widow of a former Anabaptist, with two children, a boy and a girl. It was probably his friend Farel who officiated at the ceremony. Beza described Idelette as a grave and honourable lady; Farel said she was 'not only good and honourable but also handsome'. Soon after the wedding Calvin fell severely ill—'God hastened to temper our joy', he wrote to Farel, 'so that it might not go out of bounds.' She was to him a loving and faithful wife until her death on 29 March 1549. The only child of the union survived for just two weeks. He was baptized and given the name Jacques (James). Enemies of Calvin reproached him over his childlessness. To one who brought this reproach he replied, 'The Lord gave me a child, but he was pleased to deprive me of it. In its place he has given me thousands of children in all parts of Christendom'—his spiritual sons and daughters!

In Strasbourg Calvin was the instrument in the conversion of not a few Anabaptists. Many years later, while on his deathbed, he told his colleagues how the children of Anabaptists were brought to him for baptism from many places around.

While at Strasbourg he went to colloquies between Romanists and Protestants—held under the auspices of the Emperor Charles V—at Frankfurt, Worms, and Ratisbon. If the meetings were of no avail for the reunion of Christendom (as the Emperor had hoped), they served to forge a firm friendship between Calvin and Philip Melanchthon; Calvin showed himself a friend most tender and true as steel. At the colloquies Calvin earned a name for himself by his ability in the debates; Melanchthon called him 'the theologian'. His willingness to make concessions on points to secure agreement between the various groups of Protestants was a source of surprise and sometimes of pain to some of his friends. His sketches, in letters to Farel, of the leading Romanists at the conferences—such as Eck, Luther's old antagonist—are most interesting.

To Ratisbon he had been most unwilling to go. He had small hope of good resulting. Moreover, he was in poor health, his wife was ill, and his congregation needed him, for the plague had broken out in Strasbourg. Before this he had shown that he did not fear the plague, for he had nursed Farel's nephew at Basel and ministered to him in body and soul till he died. His brethren insisted that he go to Ratisbon and, as he tells Farel, he was 'driven to go'.

The time came for his recall to Geneva. When, in 1541, he left Strasbourg after a ministry of about three years, it was with deep thankfulness in his heart for all the privileges and opportunities God had given him there. His time of preparation for his life's work at Geneva was now at an end. He was equipped as a student; he had come into touch with the Protestants of France, Italy, Switzerland, Germany, and beyond; he was the respected leader whose presence was desired at colloquies and diets; he was the friend of princes; he was without an equal among the leaders of the Reformation.

Calvin returns to Geneva.

SEVEN

REVOLUTION AT GENEVA

CALVIN WAS BANISHED from Geneva in April 1538; he returned in September 1541. The intervening period could be summed up in one word—'REVOLUTION'.

Pastors were appointed to take his place in the city. Two of them—Marcourt and Morand—are described by Martin Bucer as 'strangers to true zeal for Christ'. Two others—Pernard and de la Mare—were perhaps still worse. At any rate they did little to check the disorders of the Libertines.

The friends of the Reformers formed the party of the Guillermins (so called because Farel's Christian name was Guillaume). Among these were the pious and the learned of the city. To them Farel wrote after his departure, counselling them against hatred, recommending love and graciousness, and urging upon them the winning of fainting souls to Christ. Calvin only broke his silence on 1 October 1538, to testify his affection for them and to urge them to hope in God. The enemy, he said, was not their fellow-citizens, but the devil. He had, in other letters, spoken severely of the pastors now at Geneva; but in writing to the faithful there, he would not bring his successors into contempt. He addressed his letter to 'my well-beloved friends in our Saviour who are the remnant of the scattered Church of Geneva'.

There was now a different spirit in the Church at Geneva. He had maintained the rights of the Church; he refused to make her the servant of the State. But his successors sacrificed those rights. A Roman Catholic historian tells us that the Council and magistrates of Geneva considered the new preachers as their subjects who must render strict obedience. Doumergue tells us how this 'submission to Caesar' bore fruit in ecclesiastical and moral confusion. The college at Geneva fell into disorder and neglect, so as even to draw a remonstrance from the city of Berne; good men like Saunier and Cordier were driven away and unworthy men put in their place. The General Hospital, termed by Farel 'a fruit of the Word', was put under the control of a bankrupt who had wasted the substance of his father and of his wife and her sisters. There was also a decay of morals. On 19 February 1539, complaint was made to the Council against those singing indecent songs, blaspheming God, and running about nude. But those who had sent the aged Cordier into exile for not listening to a sermon from the new preachers, showed almost paternal benevolence towards this scandalous conduct.

In the divided state of Geneva Calvin showed the utmost moderation. The Reformation at Berne had not been as thorough as at Geneva and certain ceremonies were approved there which Calvin had not tolerated. The new pastors introduced the Bernese ceremonies and admitted all to the Lord's table without examination. Yet Calvin urged a spirit of conciliation on his friends in the city. There was increasing disorder, as even the new pastors conceded. The outlook became ever darker. Berne, though Protestant, had been guided in its relations with Geneva too much by the selfish desire to gain control of it and its adjoining districts. But Berne was now concerned over the state of affairs in Geneva. After a meeting at Morges, an agreement was reached between the pastors of Berne and Geneva—an agreement to which Calvin and Farel subscribed. The new pastors undertook (1) to acknowledge their fault in entering on the ministry in Geneva as they did; (2) not to speak against their predecessors; and (3) to remedy the decay of discipline, the neglect of the poor and of the College, with all possible faith and zeal.

On 18 March 1539, Cardinal Sadoleto, Archbishop of Carpentras, sent a letter to Geneva with the intention of winning the city back to the Roman fold. It was more or less superficial; it turned a blind eye to all the evils which flourished in the Roman Church and attributed the Reformation to the evil passions of the Reformers! The epistle, as Kampschulte, the Roman historian, tells us, gave fresh heart to the secret Romanists in the city. The Council received it courteously and promised a reply. The new pastors were not the men to answer it. The Council wanted someone with authority to answer it. After Viret refused, Calvin was asked and wrote off an answer in September. The fruit of 'a week's work', it was a devastating piece of work, which not only defended the work of the Reformation but exposed the errors of Rome, and called the Archbishop back to the faith of the fathers and apostles of the church. Calvin's *Reply to Sadoleto* was printed throughout Europe. Luther praised it. In Geneva the faithful rejoiced and the wavering were confirmed.

The party of the Reformers at Geneva stood for its political and ecclesiastical independence from Berne. The opposing party was willing to make it the vassal of Berne, and to this party most of the city Council belonged at the time of Calvin's banishment. They were called 'the Articulants', because of Articles which its representatives had signed with Berne, surrendering Genevan rights. (Because the word 'Articulant' was obsolete, the people called them 'the Artichauds' — in English the 'Artichokes'). These traitorous Articles led to a tremendous conflict. The party of the Reformers secured a majority in the Little Council of Geneva on 20 May 1540. On 5 June the three ambassadors who had signed the Articles with Berne were adjudged rebels and condemned. It was noted that of the four leaders in the city when Calvin was exiled, one was beheaded (for riot and bloodshed) and three were in flight for treason against the State. The city was almost in a condition of anarchy. Some of the new pastors sought refuge elsewhere. Geneva was threatened by Berne and by the Papacy. Who could save it? The men of the city — patriots and Protestants — thought of Calvin. On 21 September 1540, the Council commissioned one of its members, Ami Perrin, to devise some method of recalling him. This was followed by a letter from the Council. Marcourt, one of the

pastors who replaced Calvin and his friends, wrote from
Neuchâtel, urging him to accept the offer made through
the marvellous turn of events. The aged Cordier was full
of jubilant triumph over it. Viret urged Calvin with the
utmost enthusiasm to return to his children whom he had
begotten and nourished; he burned with desire to see him
revive and cheer the Genevan Church now languishing in
misery and grief.

Calvin kept silent. That silence was broken in a letter to
Farel: 'When I remember the torture I endured at Geneva,
the devouring anxiety, pardon me if I dread the place being
fatal to me.' His very soul shuddered at the thought of
return. He knew the temperament of many of the citizens,
and he foresaw difficulties with Berne. Yet, as he told Farel,
he was not seeking opportunities of escape: he desired the
good of Geneva and would hazard his life a hundred times
rather than be unfaithful to it. He replied to the Council
on 23 October. He said he had his charge at Strasbourg
and could not leave it till discharged by the Saviour 'by
some good and lawful means'; he remembered, of course,
that he had been entrusted of God with the congregation
at Geneva and felt bound to it forever. He ended his reply
without definitely accepting or refusing.

On 19 October 1540, the Council of the Two
Hundred decided to use all means to secure Calvin
as preacher. In a letter of 21 October to Farel, Calvin
set forth the reasons which made him recoil with horror from returning. He was determined to do nothing
without consulting his colleagues at Strasbourg. They
all thought he should first attend the Conference at

Worms; then on his return they would not oppose his going to Geneva. He said to Farel: 'Rather anything than return! . . . but my heart I offer to God as if slain for a sacrifice.' On the way to Worms the Genevan courier with the official recall overtook him. At the same time he had letters from Strasbourg showing how that city wanted to cling to him. He was filled with most intense emotion. He set the situation before his brethren and asked them not to think of him but of what was best for the kingdom of God. His words were mingled with sobs—more sobs than words! Twice he left them to seek repose. They advised him to keep free till after the meetings at Worms. So he sent a courteous reply to Geneva, speaking of his immediate duty at Worms and of his deference to his colleagues as if they were his parents.

After Worms he was commissioned to attend another conference — the Diet of Ratisbon. When Farel heard of this new journey, he lost all patience and poured forth his thunders. In a reply Calvin gently remonstrated with him. But the thunders proved effective: for at that time Calvin wrote to Viret: 'There is no place under heaven that I dread more (than Geneva) . . . because I see so many difficulties . . . When I think of the past . . . my heart trembles at the thought of opposing myself again to these contests': but he adds, 'I am concerned for this Church. I know not how it happens: I begin to feel more of an inclination to take the reins in hand again, if circumstances so require.' Viret, who had gone to Geneva in January 1541, at Calvin's advice, wrote to him urging his return: the hour had come for it: the votes and anxious desires of all were for him. The pastors of Zurich also wrote. They reminded him of Jonah: they begged and adjured him to go. Calvin replied to them that he dreaded this burden terribly; at the remembrance of the previous battles there, he was stiff with horror. He had a natural timidity—not for him those riots and murmurings of heresy! But Farel continued to thunder: 'Are you waiting till the stones cry out? I think you are stone enough yourself to reject so impiously the entreaties of this Church.' With supreme patience Calvin replied that he would go: 'I will go soon. You cannot ask more of me, unless perhaps you take pleasure in overwhelming me with your complaints.' In his Preface to his *Commentary on the Psalms* Calvin says:

> Necessity was imposed upon me of returning to my former charge, contrary to my desire and inclination. The welfare of this Church, it is true, lay so near my heart, that for its sake I would not have hesitated to lay down my life; but my timidity nevertheless suggested to me many reasons for excusing myself for again willingly taking on my shoulders so heavy a burden. At length, however, a solemn and conscientious regard to my duty prevailed with me to consent to return to the flock from which I had been torn; but with what grief, tears, great anxiety and distress I did this, the Lord is my best witness.

Furnished with letters from the pastors at Strasbourg (dated 1 September 1541) for Basel, Berne, and Geneva, he set out. The Council of Strasbourg still pled that he might have opportunity to return to them. On 13

September 1541, he re-entered Geneva. The great Council had repealed the sentence of banishment and a mounted herald had been sent to fetch him. He had no retinue with him—not even Farel! Yet it was more than the entry of a prince or an emperor, for he was going to make the city the capital of a greater realm than an Alexander or a Charlemagne had ever dreamed of—an empire of souls. There was indeed a feeling in the heart of Bucer and in the hearts of the men of Zurich that in taking charge of Geneva he was taking charge of all the churches. It had a central position—it lay at the door of France, Italy, Switzerland, and Germany.

Beza tells us that he received a great welcome from all the people and from the Senate. Immediately he presented himself before the Council, excused himself for his delay, and asked that order might be established in the Church. He had resumed his duty.

The period of preparation was over. He had acquired a store of knowledge of the truth and of the Christian world. Fourteen years of struggle at Geneva, followed by nine years of triumph, lay ahead. He was the instrument of God for the task, the servant of the Almighty. His heart was a sacrifice on the altar of God.

EIGHT

GENEVA IN CALVIN'S TIME

IN those days men journeyed on horseback. Wheeled carriages were only beginning to be used in the middle of the 16th century. Calvin, writing to Beza on 19 November 1561, speaks of mounting his horse to go to dinner. The inns and hostelries of Geneva were heated by stoves. Calvin could not bear the fumes of these—they gave him severe headaches. Fortunately, to the fumes of the stoves there was not added the smoke of tobacco. Tobacco was not introduced (into France) till 1556 or 1559. Pope Urban VIII excommunicated smokers in 1624. James I of England wrote against them too. The Jesuits declared themselves in favour of tobacco. Emile Doumergue, Calvin's biographer, says that the Reformer doubtless never even heard of tobacco.

The beds in the inns were arranged as in a dormitory. Montaigne, a much younger contemporary of Calvin, speaks of an inn at Baden with 170 beds, 17 stoves, and 11 kitchens catering for 300 persons. This hotel had some single rooms, which was unusual for those times.

Imagine yourself sitting down at a meal in an inn in

Geneva. First, you must remove your hat for the prayer. The hotel-keeper must be careful as to this prayer, for it was laid down that grace must be said before and after each meal. The prayer over, you replace your hat for the meal. (In fact, the pastors wore their hats while preaching in the pulpit.) The table is square, and you are seated on a bench or a wooden chair. On the table there is a cloth. We hope it is clean. Erasmus, writing some fifty years earlier, speaks of cloths in hostelries which went unwashed for six months! There are no serviettes; they had not yet come into use; they began to be used in France in the eighteenth century, but not till later in Germany or Italy. The fringe of the table-cloth must suffice for wiping oneself!

On the table before you there is a wooden trencher on which you are to carve your meat. There are plates of wood and tin in use also.

The rules of etiquette in the 16th century differed vastly from those of our day. Even in the 17th century we find a Duke of Austria, when his nobility were dining with him, laying down the following rules: 'Not to put the hand in the dish; not to throw bones behind you or under the table; not to lick one's fingers nor spit on the plate, nor to wipe one's nose on the table-cloth.'

On the table there would be an abundance of spices, for the men of the 16th century were fond of cinnamon, ginger, pepper, cloves and the like. They had strange tastes. For example, they put the juice of sour grapes in their soup.

Forks were not in use in those days. A book of etiquette dating back to 1483 prescribed that food was to be taken with three fingers. Years later—after Calvin's time—

Montaigne was still eating with his fingers, and he rather fancied himself to be a gentleman! 'Calvin had no fork; he ate with his fingers', Doumergue tells us. And Doumergue a little later in his record adds: 'The Reformers—Zwingli, Oecolampadius, Bullinger, Myconius—and Calvin and Farel and Viret—ate with their fingers, without forks, and even on occasion invoking the aid of their knives!'

At the beginning of the Reformation Geneva was a beautiful city, for it was then a city of open spaces. There were gardens and orchards and barns, and the houses were usually no more than three stories high. The transformation began about 1534 when Geneva became a place of refuge. An exodus of men, women and children from France and other lands where they were in peril on account of their faith, began arriving in the city. They came through rocky defiles, avoiding known paths. They came in the snow and bitter cold—famished, destitute and utterly weary. When they saw the Lake of Geneva and the towers of St Peter's where Calvin preached, they broke into tears and sobs of joy; men and women pressed their children to their breasts with gladness of heart. They had reached the city of peace, where they might enjoy the liberty of the gospel.

To house the homeless refugees two courses were pursued. More houses were built in the suburbs, in the gardens and orchards, and along the lanes linking one street to another. So there also arose great blocks of houses.

When no more room on the ground was available, they expanded upwards. They raised their houses higher and higher still. So old quarters of the city, which had been most beautiful, gave place to narrow and dark streets, with dwellings where twelve or fifteen families were crowded together in the one abode. This led to a sad disfigurement of the city, but that disfigurement was its glory. It was love for the persecuted that brought it about. A city of 13,000 people received, housed, and fed about 12,000 refugees in the relatively short period of Calvin's ministry. It took great effort and involved much expense, for the refugees came starving and with only the clothes they were wearing.

The families of Geneva previous to this time had maintained their privacy, with a certain aloofness to strangers. Now all this was changed. The city's gates were opened wide. Beds were put everywhere, sometimes five or six in a room, and with as many as forty-five people living in a house. The houses in Calvin's time in Geneva were simply furnished—for the same reason as their streets were dark and their houses high. It was a religious and political camp, a city of refuge. There was no place for luxury and ease; all was austerity and sacrifice. Its men were soldiers ready to bear arms at a moment's notice in defence of their wives, their children and their firesides. They must continually be on the alert, for were not Savoy and France and Spain threatening them on every side, looking for an opportunity to seize their city? No wonder the chief adornment of their homes was the pike, the cuirass, the hauberk,[1] hanging on the walls. The chief adornment? No, not quite. The chief place must be reserved for the Bible, the sword of

---

[1] Cuirass: a defensive breastplate and backplate fastened together: a breastplate alone. Hauberk: a long coat of chain-mail sometimes ending in short trousers: originally armour for the neck.

the Spirit, the believer's shield and buckler. At one stage there was a feverish activity on the part of the men of Geneva to make and repair their fortifications; and it is reported that Calvin himself took shovel in hand to raise the mound of defence against the foe.

In spite of all the threats, Geneva stood fast by the grace of God. It stood fast, for it was founded on a rock. It not only stood fast; it was a strength and a source of blessing to the Protestant world, sending a Knox to Scotland, a Peter Martyr to England, and a Marnix to the Low Countries.

In the matter of morals, there was a wonderful change wrought in Geneva in the course of the years of Calvin's ministry. Before the advent of the Reformation, the Roman Church had put no great restraint upon vice, and so immorality reigned. The Reformation replaced licence with discipline. The moral laws of the Christian life were proclaimed. Riotous feasting was strictly regulated; measures were taken to reform the abounding evils of the taverns of the time. Bonivard tells us that in 1517—before the advent of the Reformation—the city was given over to worldly pleasure, to card-games, to dances and feasts and wantonness and noise and strife. Under the ministry of the Word, Geneva became a city of God. The Word was preached five times on a Sunday and on week-days there were also sermons and lectures. And the citizens were vigorously encouraged to attend on the ministry of the pulpit.

On the walls of the city of Geneva was the motto IHS —the first three letters of the name Jesus (in the Greek). It was not a mere motto, as so often happens with inscriptions of this kind. Calvin sought to make it a meaningful motto—full of meaning for every citizen. Geneva, he said, must be the holy Jerusalem.

Church of St Peter, Geneva.

NINE

POOR OR RICH?

GREAT AND DEVOUT CROWDS filled the Church of St Peter's to hear Calvin preach, even as early as five o'clock on summer mornings and six o'clock in winter. St Peter's in his day was plain and unadorned, but the numbers thronging it were far greater than at the ornate Roman services held there before the Reformation. In fact the church became too small, and to meet the need the number of services was increased, and there were services on weekdays as well as on Sabbaths. All the magistrates of the city were present every Sabbath. As Calvin preached, a secretary took down his sermons and lectures, and many of them were printed and went forth to nourish fellow-believers in many lands.

In this church there were some stirring scenes. Here on 3 September 1553, Calvin covered the symbols of bread and wine with his hands and offered to die rather than give the elements to the profane Libertines who were pushing boldly forward to receive them. From this pulpit on 5 June 1559, he spoke in the presence of the city magistrates and pastors and 600 scholars, when the famous College and

Academy of Geneva were established. Here the voice of mourning rose over the massacre of St Bartholomew's Day in France; here also was heard the voice of thanksgiving for marvellous deliverances and victories of the Protestant cause.

The voice of calumny was raised against Calvin in his own day and has often been raised since. The charge has been brought that he used his unique position in Geneva to 'feather his own nest'. Actually, his salary of 500 florins (plus twelve hundredweights of flour and two measures of wine) was very moderate, and he refused any increase. True, but his enemies say that he received many gifts. Even supposing this were true, it is also true that he had many expenses as well. He was not a pastor of the Genevan Church alone; he was the most influential spokesman for the Reformed churches in Switzerland and elsewhere in Europe. He had the expenses of a vast correspondence, and correspondence was much more elaborate and time-consuming than it is today. At times he had travelling expenses, and he incurred a heavy cost to care for the poor and refugees. It is perhaps interesting to note that the poor box at the church door—that innovation of the Protestant Church—was not introduced in Geneva till 1568, four years after Calvin's death. There is no doubt that he gave freely to the poor from his own pocket while he lived. He kept open house for all comers. He found this difficult on his moderate income, for he tells Viret in 1549 that he could scarcely make ends meet, on account of 'the heavy burden of passers-by'.

In January 1546 the Council of Geneva was informed

of 'the sickness of M. Calvin who has no resources'. They sent him ten crowns but he refused them. So it was no wonder that later in the month, when he was having a discussion with an Anabaptist before the Council, and the Anabaptist called him avaricious, the whole Council burst out laughing. They knew of his recent refusal and of his returning part of his salary. The presents given him during his long ministry in Geneva were almost all either refused or paid for. He also refused, during his last illness, the quarterly salary which was brought him. He had not earned it, he said, so how could he accept it?

In reply to the lies spread by the Romanists during his life-time he said, 'My death at all events will show that I have not been a money-making man.' It was reported that he had bought a property. Actually, he did not own a foot of ground. In 1547 he could write that he had not a house of his own. He said he had not enough to buy an acre except when his quarterly salary came. Theodore Beza testifies that at his death his whole estate, including 'the proceeds of his library', did not exceed a few hundred gold pieces. His biographer, Felix Bungener, says that Pope Pius IV, on hearing of his death, said of him: 'That which made the strength of that heretic was that money was nothing to him.'

For all his literary activity he received no remuneration. He was a great, disinterested man, and though he had the opportunity of becoming rich, especially in his later years when he was so widely honoured and respected, he died in comparative poverty. There are plenty of testimonies to the simplicity of his life and his contempt for the riches of the world. He wished, he said, for no more than his daily needs required. Even this he had not always. For years he contented himself with a single meal in the day.

The *Rue des Chanoines* (the street of the Canons) where he lived is today *Rue Calvin*. His house no longer remains, but the courtyard and garden are still to be seen. Though the house has gone, there is a list of the furniture lent him by the City Council. It shows that the house was not sumptuously furnished—it was provided with the bare necessities.

One day a stranger knocked at his door. It was none other than the old enemy of Geneva, whose attack Calvin had answered so devastatingly—Cardinal Sadoleto. He was travelling *incognito* and desired to see Calvin. He was not the only cardinal who wished to see him. Calvin tells Viret in 1553 of a Cardinal du Bellay who was passing through Geneva and proposed to call on him, but he was not at home. 'I think he did not greatly wish to have conversation with me', said Calvin. When Sadoleto arrived he thought he would find him in a palace or magnificent mansion, with numerous attendants. He was therefore greatly surprised when directed to such a small and inconspicuous abode. In answer to his knock Calvin himself, simply attired, opened the door. The Cardinal was utterly astonished and voiced his amazement. No doubt Calvin was rather astonished too when the stranger made himself known!

TEN

CALVIN'S TOILS

CALVIN'S HOUSE IN GENEVA was one of the busiest of workshops. He took little sleep and ate sparingly. 'In diet he was temperate', says his biographer, Theodore Beza, 'being equally averse to sordidness and luxury.' Dr Mitchell Hunter says of Calvin's literary labours:

> From the time he took up his pen to write the *Institutes* till he laid it down eight hours before he breathed his last, it was seldom idle . . . With such impetuosity and rush did he often dictate that his secretary could scarcely keep up with him. Charles de Jonviller, to whom Calvin latterly dictated his letters, tells us that in taking them down he was often 'overcome with admiration at the singular eloquence that he poured forth'.

Calvin worked into the night and was at his desk at dawn again after his morning devotions. Even when forced to recline on his bed during the day, for his health's sake, he was busy dictating to some scribe. He had a marvellous memory. If he was interrupted in his dictation, as happened frequently, he could resume hours later, without any aid, at the point where he had left off.

Every other week he preached daily before a discerning audience; he frequently preached twice on Sundays; every week he gave three lectures before 'doctors of the law' and students of the Word: every week he discoursed before the full assembly on a Scripture passage. Beside these, there were monthly discussions, meetings of the Consistory, and so on. Moreover, he was consulted on everything, and was always in demand.

If no man laboured so, no man was more disturbed. One day a man presented himself claiming to have received a revelation from God — he was 'Moses', Calvin was 'Aaron'. On another day a disturbance was caused by a rascal called Alberg to whom the Reformer had at one time given money — money which he could little afford and had to borrow from another source. Alberg deposited a box with Calvin as a pledge for the loan. In the course of time, when the Reformer learned of Alberg's untrustworthy character from others, the box, given in pledge, was duly opened and was found to contain a few worthless old books, 'tattered and torn' and a few 'mouldy apples'. Later when news reached Calvin of Alberg's arrival in Basel, the Reformer returned the box, having replaced everything in it, 'not without much laughter'! Calvin, reporting all this to his friend Oswald Myconius, adds: 'The rascal, having received it, went about proclaiming that I was a thief, that I had taken out of it many incomparable books.' When Alberg arrived in Geneva, Calvin 'told him he was a most impudent scoundrel'. But that was not the end of the matter. 'The day after he attacked me in my own house, not only with the most abusive language, but also making a furious assault; hereupon he was given into custody.'[1]

Another day another disturbance; this time by an unprincipled fellow named Baudoin, to whom Calvin in his guilelessness gave hospitality. He was repaid by the theft of some of his papers, which Baudoin later sought to use against him.

There were so many interruptions that Calvin could not get two hours free at a stretch. On 21 August 1547, he wrote to Viret saying that he was so burdened with continual correspondence—much of it quite laborious—that he was almost wearied of life itself. On the same date he wrote to Farel: 'I have not even an hour free—amid continual interruptions.' Sometimes there were more than twenty interruptions in the course of writing a single letter! In 1554 he excused himself to Farel saying, 'At the moment I have not time to write. The hour of my lecture is come, and I have not been able yet to think on what I shall say.' Although his correspondence fills many volumes, we probably have only about half of it—about 4,000 letters.[2]

Geneva was the heart and centre of the Reformed churches of all lands, and Calvin's home in the *Rue des Chanoines* was the centre of Geneva. It was no dark and gloomy abode. Professor Doumergue gives it four titles:—

1. An Inn of Friendship. Calvin had a welcome for all comers. His friends Farel and Viret he especially delighted to entertain. To his house Viret comes to be nursed when

[1] John Calvin, *Tracts and Letters,* vol. 4, pp. 317-19.
[2] Out of this large number of letters, 600 were carefully selected, for their historical importance and spiritual value, and were first published in the 19th century. See volumes 4-7 of John Calvin, *Tracts and Letters.*

ill; and when he is mourning he is invited, with the utmost tenderness, to return. It is good to know that this great man was not always studying and working. He played quoits in the garden or a 'game of keys' indoors. This game consisted in shoving a key over the surface of a long table to see who could push his key nearest the far edge. When a key fell over the edge after a light and last touch, there were bursts of laughter from the onlookers. These Reformers could laugh loud into their long pointed beards! There is often the note of laughter or of pleasantry in Calvin's writings.

2. A Post Office. To Calvin's house came bearers of letters from every land and in all kinds of dress. They had seen the correspondents and were often regarded as their trusted confidants. They came with a store of information, and so they were brought in, questioned, and conversed with. Calvin's house was therefore like an 'information bureau' to which news came from such lands as England, Poland, and even Russia. In those days when there were no newspapers, with what eagerness pastors and members of the City Council hurried to his house for the latest news, especially when important events were transpiring, or when important issues were at stake in the outside world. One historian refers to Calvin as 'the foreign minister of Geneva', and such a description is not far from the truth. In fact, when delicate political negotiations were being carried on, not only did the Council of Geneva appeal to Calvin for aid, the Council of Berne even committed matters into his hands.

3. A Registry Office. Calvin suggests a servant for Farel; he sends a secretary to Viret. Well-to-do families in Geneva often wished to send their children to Zurich to learn German, and families in other cities desired to send their children to Geneva for instruction. Children came to Geneva even from distant Poland, and were committed into the care of Calvin. He often made arrangements in such cases. His letters bear testimony that he loved some of these children as if they were his very own, and there is evidence that they reciprocated his affection.

One of the commonest requests which came to him from other lands was for the provision of pastors and teachers. Such a request came from far away Russia.

4. A Matrimonial Agency. The Protestants were scattered—living often in the midst of foes. There could be no mixed marriages—this would be perilous to the cause. So it was not only for his friend Viret, but for many others also, that Calvin was anxious to secure a good wife. His letters show that he knew the eligible ladies of his town and of the surrounding country, and even of other towns such as Neuchâtel. He knew their dowry, their training, and whether or not they were pretty. The defender of the mysteries of predestination, the incomparable worker and scholar, was also intensely practical and intensely down-to-earth.

As Calvin's position grew more commanding and his influence more far-reaching, greater demands were made upon him. But he laboured on, ever under the great Taskmaster's eye.

Calvin's garden, Geneva.

ELEVEN

———————

CALVIN'S FRAILTIES AND CHARM

PROFESSOR EMILE DOUMERGUE says that the extraordinary labours of Calvin resulted in an extraordinary series of maladies. 'It would be easier', he says, 'to recount the diseases Calvin did not have than those of which he became the prey. He passed a life of simplicity and labour in the *Rue des Chanoines:* but he passed there especially a life of suffering—suffering the continuity and intensity of which is absolutely exceptional, startling, prodigious.'

Theodore Beza tells us:

> His diseases, the effects of incredible exertions of body and mind, were various and complicated. Besides being naturally of a feeble and spare body, inclining to consumption, he slept almost waking, and spent a great part of the year in preaching, lecturing, and dictating. For at least ten years he . . . took no food at all till supper; so that it is wonderful he could have so long escaped consumption. Being subject to hemicrania, for which starvation was the only cure, he in consequence sometimes abstained from food for thirty-six hours

in succession . . . He became afflicted with ulcerated haemorrhoids, and occasionally for about five years before his death discharged considerable quantities of blood. When the quartan fever left him, his right limb was seized with gout; every now and then he had attacks of colic, and last of all he was afflicted with the stone . . . The physicians used what remedies they could and there was no man who attended more carefully to the prescriptions of his physicians, except that in regard to mental exertions he was most careless of his health, not even his headaches preventing him from taking his turn in preaching. While oppressed with so many diseases, no man ever heard him utter a word unbecoming a man of firmness, far less unbecoming a Christian.

Felix Bungener sums up the illnesses which beset Calvin thus:

Pains in his head, pains in his legs, pains in his stomach, spitting of blood, difficulty in breathing, the gout, the stone—*in fine,* nothing was wanting to his long torture, which was scarcely interrupted by a few days less intolerable.

A Genevan physician of note, Dr Gautier, sums up in the pages of Doumergue's *Calvin* the history of Calvin's sicknesses as follows:

Calvin was a good type of the sufferer from arthritis. The series of manifestations of this morbid predisposition was in his case almost complete: migraine, dyspepsia, haemorrhoids, gravel, gout . . . It almost seems as if we were reading through Bouchard's treatise on the diseases of malnutrition . . . Two super-added episodes cast spots on this picture of otherwise uniform tint; the intermittent fever and the pulmonary symptoms. Intermittent fever is now very rare in Geneva. It was probably much more frequent when the town was surrounded by muddy ditches. It is also possible that Calvin contracted it on one of his journeys. Up to the 16th century all the countries of Europe were in this respect nearly as unhealthy as the tropical countries are now.

. . . As to the pulmonary symptoms, I think we may unhesitatingly share Blaurer's view that Calvin was a complete consumptive. But Calvin was arthritic; he was even gouty . . . And the arthritic, especially if he be actually gouty, presents a bad soil for tuberculosis. The consumption therefore developed slowly with the Reformer. It was shut up to producing from time to time some blood-spitting or an attack of suffocating bronchitis. I do not believe that Calvin succumbed to an advancing consumption. It is more likely that he was carried away by infection of the urinary tract, following upon gravel. Arthritis therefore lies at the root of nearly all Calvin's sicknesses; but on the other hand he fully fed this tendency. His sedentary habits, his devouring mental activity, his daily cares for the work and for the churches were the elements of a deplorable hygiene. If he could have consulted a present-day physician, he would have prescribed rest, freedom from anxiety, life in the open air in the country, and a diet almost exclusively of milk and vegetables. He followed the opposite course, happily for his work, but unhappily for the length and comfort of his life. But if this temperament filled the Reformer's life with almost continual sufferings, there is also another side of the matter which should not be passed over. If arthritis has its drawbacks, it has also its advantages. It is the nervous arthritics who have left behind them the traces of their sojourn on earth. Their faculties are more developed, their will stronger, their energy more intense, than in the case of men of a different constitution and of less highly tempered fibre. If the son of the cooper of Noyon had been born lymphatic and scrofulous, there would probably have been no occasion for writing the life of John Calvin.

When we think of the vast amount of work done by this sufferer whose body was like a walking hospital, we may well be astounded. He has been charged, as we have already hinted, with irritability. Beza admits that he was naturally of a keen temper and that this was heightened by the laborious life he led. The wonder is that this sick, overwrought man was not more irritable by far, especially under the strong provocations to which he was often subject. But Beza tells us that 'the Spirit of the Lord had so taught him to command his anger that no word was heard to proceed from him unbecoming a good man.'

What lay behind the mighty influence Calvin wielded? His genius, his activity, his teaching, his eloquence, and his sympathy explain much, but they do not explain all with regard to the power he exercised over thousands of hearts. Doumergue says: 'We do not capture men or nations (or even flies) with vinegar and gall: we must have honey.' Yes, there was 'honey'. True, there was an austerity about Calvin—a gravity. There was even at times an irritability—a natural irritability sharpened by debilitating sicknesses. But it cannot be gainsaid that he had a wonderful charm—a wonderful attractiveness of character. Beza testifies that though he seemed grave, yet among friends in familiar surroundings none could be more pleasant than he. In his youth in France this was abundantly evident. It was also shown in the few weeks of his stay in Italy. But it was in the *Rue des Chanoines* at Geneva that his charm was particularly powerful over the hearts of men.

He had a capacity for friendship; and even though he was much engaged in great affairs, he had the faculty of neglecting no detail in the lives of his friends and correspondents. A friend wrote to him about the laziness of one of his boys. Another wrote to tell him that he had donned the matrimonial 'muzzle'. His correspondents felt sure that the man of Geneva was interested in all their news.

The son of Justus Jonas (Luther's friend) enjoyed Calvin's friendship and spoke of him as 'our Calvin'—a man dearer to him than his own soul. Another wrote with gratitude of the marks of kindness shown him by the Reformer during a visit to Geneva, and said, 'I am convinced that you seek the interest of those from whom you can hope for no return and that your kindness to them surpasses all they could have wished for, even in their dreams.' Such was his reputation that men came from every land to meet him, to see his church, and to receive some comfort from him.

Calvin was indeed a man of a very tender heart. 'You know', he wrote to Pierre Viret, 'how very tender my heart is, or, I should better say soft.' And Viret replied, 'Yes, I know how tender a heart you have.' He wrote to Martin Bucer, 'If on any point, I do not make response as you hoped, you know I am in your power; reprove, rebuke, do all that a father can to a son.' And Bucer, a year later, responded by addressing him as 'My heart! my soul!'

There are letters in abundance to show that Calvin exercised this tremendous charm even to the very close of his life, when he was desperately weak and ill. Even one who was by no means an enthusiastic Calvinist bore this testimony: 'It is certain that Calvin exercised on those who visited him an irresistible ascendancy.'

Peter Viret (1511-1571)

TWELVE

BUILDING THE WALLS OF ZION

IN THE PRECEDING CHAPTERS we have dealt with the Geneva of Calvin, the times in which he lived, the man himself and his preparation for his great task, and the ailments which hampered him. Now we set out to survey the twenty-three years of his ministry at Geneva following upon his return from exile—fourteen years of struggle followed by nine years of triumph.

Calvin returned 'amid the congratulations of the whole people', Theodore Beza tells us. His recall was an acknowledgment of the insult done to God and his Word in the sentence of exile. But when Calvin re-entered the pulpit of St Peter's, he had not a word to say of the past or of the reversal of fortune. After a few sentences on the manner in which he intended to fulfil his duties, he immediately began to explain the Scriptures where he had left off some years before—just as if he had been only momentarily interrupted!

He appeared before the Council on 1 September 1541, to urge the setting up of a Consistory composed of elders and pastors—with power to exercise discipline. The first meeting of this court was on the 8 December 1541. The task ahead was simply tremendous. It was to rebuild an edifice which lay in ruins. He acted with the greatest care. He tolerated for a time what he could not change. This man who often bewailed his impatience showed a most singular moderation.

The first need of discipline was among the ranks of his colleagues in the ministry. Instead of being helps, they were hindrances. Two of them had been there before his return and they had shown themselves the ready vassals of the State. They had no love for the order and discipline introduced by Calvin. They were ignorant and presumptuous rather than zealous for the truth. Calvin leaned greatly on his faithful colleague Peter Viret. If this support were withdrawn, he felt he would be altogether overwhelmed. Yet Viret returned to Lausanne on the 16 July 1542. Calvin received new colleagues. Of the four appointed, two were most disappointing. There were quarrels among them. He warned, rebuked, and exhorted them, but all to no purpose. 'What colleagues! what difficulties!' exclaims Professor Emile Doumergue.

Then came the trouble with Sebastian Castellio. Castellio had professed conversion through reading Calvin's *Institutes*. He came to Calvin at Strasbourg and lived with him for a time. When Calvin reorganised the College at Geneva after his return, Castellio was installed as Principal on 7 June 1542. He resigned his charge in 1543 without any valid reason. He wished to be recognised as a pastor, but Calvin declared that he held an opinion which rendered him unsuitable. Even those who are opposed to Calvin admit that Castellio was of an unsettled and contentious character. Eventually the ministers gave Castellio a certificate which was drawn up by Calvin and signed by him in the name of all. It begins by declaring that Castellio of his own free-will gave up the office of Principal, and goes on to say that when they asked him if he was in accord with them on all points of doctrine, he mentioned two points of difference. The first point was about the Lord's 'Descent into Hell' mentioned in the Apostles' Creed. An understanding could perhaps have been reached on this point; but the second point brought to light a more serious disagreement. Castellio esteemed the Song of Solomon to be an impure and lascivious love-song. They did all they could to lead him to the truth, pointing out similarities between the Song and Psalm 45. The unanimous decision of the pastors was that it would form a dangerous precedent to appoint as pastor a man who openly rejected a book which was reckoned by all the churches to be part of God's inspired Word. He had worthily fulfilled his duties as Principal, and it was not because of any blemish upon his life or of any wicked doctrine that he had been refused admission to the ministry. Castellio set out for Lausanne and Calvin recommended him to Viret, urging that silence be maintained as to his views on the disputed points and that Viret help him as far as he could. Calvin shows how well-disposed he was to Castellio, but he would have wished him possessed of a sounder judgment and a deeper humility. Castellio had appeared at one of Calvin's Friday meetings and had thrown fierce and indiscriminate charges against the pastors. Calvin did not wish to engage in sharp discussion before strangers, and carried the matter before the magistrates. They urged the putting away of all rancour and rebuked Castellio. A month later he withdrew from Geneva, but he seemed to bear a grudge against Calvin ever after.

There were some who wished to be pastors, whose admission to the office Calvin resisted on the ground of their unsuitability. Others showed themselves unworthy and had to be dismissed from office — five of them between 1542 and 1546. At last he had the satisfaction of seeing better men in the ministry; from 1546 his colleagues were worthy men who were of one mind with him.

He had his troubles with the Council. They were not sympathetic to all his efforts and to his high standards. He suffered many affronts from them. They sometimes went further than he wished. He was personally in favour of the abolition of certain feast-days which were kept at Berne and which had been introduced at Geneva during his exile. But he was willing for the sake of accord with Berne to have a service for worship on these days, provided the people were free to return to their work when the service was over. For a time he sought to put this into practice but he soon felt compelled to complain to the Council about the diversity of practice — some opened their shops on these days, others kept them closed. He appealed to the Council to secure some uniformity. After he had left the Council-chamber, the Council resolved to abolish the feast days altogether. Though surprised by their action, he saw no reason to contest the point. Some of his foes sought to involve him with Berne on this question. He wrote to Berne to explain how the decision was reached.

Amid his toils and difficulties he was occupied with every-day affairs—with rents and purchases and repairs and marriages. He looks for a house for Monsieur de Falais, and he makes the estimate for its repair himself. He gives advice as to a proposal of marriage. He was busy with weddings and with baptisms. He writes to Farel of a gown which he is awaiting an opportunity of sending to him. He writes a long letter of many pages to the Almoner of the Duchess of Ferrara. He writes recommendations for those seeking work. Men said of Samuel Rutherford that he was 'always preaching, always visiting the sick, always writing and studying'. The same might have been said of Calvin, and it was especially his preaching which conquered Geneva at last. For well over twenty years he was a prodigy in their midst. The Consistory met every week, and he appeared regularly before the Council. In the council-chamber he delivered many an address and many an appeal, usually *impromptu*, often with glowing and impetuous eloquence leaving his adversaries dumb, often with tact and moderation and winsomeness, often with the biting and crushing retort of which he was master. His memory was like a travelling library, from which he could draw 'with both hands'.

There were difficulties with Berne and these led to months of negotiation. Calvin used all his influence for a peaceful settlement. If his advice had been taken at the first, the affair would have been settled at once. As it was, it was only after months of debate that his counsel finally prevailed. Yet instead of being grateful, the Council sought to go their way without his aid. But further trouble with Berne arose; Geneva wished to raise its tolls to fill its empty coffers, but Berne was violently opposed to this action. The Council sought Calvin's help in drawing up a reply; but the reply sent was too strong for his liking.

The plague visited the city in 1542. Calvin was willing, if need be, to act as chaplain at the plague hospital, but the Council forbade him. Two of his colleagues who volunteered for this duty died of the infectious disease.

He wrote, at the urgent request of Farel, refuting the views of the Anabaptists. He spoke of this sect as a pernicious plague. 'We are delivered from the law of the letter', they said; and they declared the writers of the New Testament to be carnal.

He was occupied not only with matters great and small at Geneva and its neighbourhood; he had at heart the interests of the kingdom of God everywhere. In November 1544, he had written to Heinrich Bullinger praising the pure and simple *Confession of Faith of the Vaudois of Provence*. On 4 May 1545, he described the fierce persecution which the king of France let loose upon them, burning them in barns and wiping out whole villages. Only 4,000 escaped to wander in the mountains. Calvin urged that these faithful Christians be assisted. He worked with all his might for their relief. Farel and he visited Berne, Basle, Zurich, and Strasbourg to concert efforts on their behalf.

In 1549 he and Farel made a visit to Zurich which resulted in the drawing up of the statement known as the *Consensus Tigurinus*. In two hours agreement was reached. This confession aimed at setting forth the truth clearly without disguise or guile; it was sent to all the Swiss Churches and agreed to by all. The unity of the Protestant Churches, Calvinist and Zwinglian, was made clear. This brought great joy to Calvin. He told Bullinger of Zurich that the concord between them had helped to ease the burden of his grief over the death of his wife which had taken place some months before. John Calvin had a truly ecumenical heart.

Heinrich Bullinger (1504-1575).

A sixteenth century portrait of Calvin.

THIRTEEN

CALVIN VERSUS THE LIBERTINES

IN THE EARLY PART OF 1546, just four years after Calvin's return to Geneva, an open struggle with the Libertines broke out. The Libertines were a group of patriotic, old Genevan families who had led the republic to independence and the reformation. But they grew to deeply resent the dominant influence of Calvin and 'foreigners' in the affairs of their city. From 1546 till 1555 their struggle with Calvin became increasingly bitter. Felix Bungener says: 'Nine years he [Calvin] was every moment on the point of being—not conquered, for he was not of those who can be conquered, but—crushed: for nine years it was his to expect every month and every week to be expelled from that city which he was nevertheless continuing to render illustrious and powerful abroad; for nine years he guided Geneva as a vessel on fire which burns the captain's feet and yet obeys him, and which in combat is not less formidable and feared.' Let us look at some of the Libertine leaders.

Pierre Ameaux, a member of the Little Council of Geneva, was a maker of playing-cards. He lost part of his trade because of the city ordinances against card-playing. He was annoyed too with the Consistory for not facilitating his divorce, though this was at last granted by the Council—after eighteen months of disputing. His wife was a woman whose 'spiritual libertinism' was little else than another name for vice. On 27 January 1546, Ameaux invited four friends to dine with him. Before them he inveighed against Calvin, his doctrine and his authority, saying that he was a wicked seducer, that he wished to be bishop, and that if they were not careful these Frenchmen would rule the city. His friends informed against him before the Council. He was put in prison. He first denied making the remark attributed to him, then admitted it and acknowledged that he had maligned and slandered the pastors. The pastors as a body insisted that he be dealt with. The Council ordered that he make public apology, bareheaded and with torch in hand as the custom was, in three public places in the city. But there is clear evidence that Calvin did not wish too great severity to be shown toward him.

One leading family of Libertines—the Favres—played a great part in the struggles of these few years. Francis Favre, a draper, when brought before the Consistory in February 1547, and questioned, refused to answer; he objected to the 'French' pastors and to their yoke of discipline. He was guilty of gross immorality but was quite brazen about it. In 1546 he had told the Consistory that he did not recognise the pastors. One of Calvin's colleagues, Abel Poupin, said that they did not recognise him as one of Christ's sheep, but as a dog. The men of the 16th century did not mince their words! Jeeringly, Francis went about everywhere grinding his teeth and saying, 'I am a dog.' After eighteen days in prison he begged for mercy and quitted Geneva for a time.

At the end of 1545 Gaspard, son of Francis Favre, was put in prison. Again he was imprisoned for a few days in March the following year. On his release he was questioned as to whether he had stated that if he became a magistrate he would set up places of debauchery in the city. He denied the allegation. At Easter 1546, he pretended to play at skittles during the sermon. He was taken to task but was quite bold about it. He left the city for nearly two years. After his return he engaged in more strife and was put in prison. On the day he came out he went to have sport before St Peter's while Calvin was preaching. Calvin's lecture was interrupted by the uproar made by Gaspard and his friends. The next year he was imprisoned for his immorality.

Gaspard's sister, Frances, was married to Ami Perrin, who was first the friend and then the foe of Calvin. Frances was a fury of a woman. Those who opposed her would be sure to feel the lash of her tongue, if not the blows of her fists! She was fond of the dance; but she used her feet too on her own relations. On one occasion when her mother-in-law came to call, she speeded her departure with 'a good kick'. On another occasion, while coming out of prison and leaving the city, she met Abel Poupin, insulted him, crashed against him with her horse and rode on. Calvin called her Penthesilea, after the Queen of the Amazons.

The chief leader of the Libertines was Ami Perrin. Theodore Beza tells us that he was 'an exceedingly foolish but daring and ambitious man'. He was dubbed by Calvin 'the comic Caesar'—because of his vanity and his ambitious pretensions. He was accused of having secret negotiations with France, and was deposed from his offices of member of Council and Captain-general. He was not as evil as the Favres and was no traitor, but his factiousness and his vanity made him dangerous. His colleagues in the leadership of the Libertines were Vandel and Berthelier. They stirred up great tumults at times. On one occasion, before a meeting of the Council of the Two Hundred, there were loud shouts and a confused clamour outside the chamber. Calvin, who arrived a little early for the meeting, saw that sedition was afoot and that blood was about to be shed. The sight was dreadful, he said. He rushed among the combatants and offered his body to their swords. He told them to begin with him. He spoke with such dignity and self-possession that the tumult at once subsided.

In the Council room it broke out afresh—they were 'on the point of drawing their swords and staining the court itself with mutual slaughter', records Beza. Through Calvin's intervention yet again a dreadful carnage was averted. He then delivered a long and eloquent discourse that deeply moved nearly all his hearers. Even Perrin gave the Reformer his hand and promised to repent. But Calvin was under no illusion; he felt that his hearer was a 'deaf' man. Early in 1548—partly by the intervention of Farel and Viret—Perrin was restored to some of his dignity and there was the promise of peace; but the disturbances broke out afresh. Calvin's burden seemed too great to bear. He could be pardoned if at times he longed to escape to some haven of peace. These opponents of his really hated the gospel; they were lewd and dissolute, and the gospel was a curb on their moral laxity.

On 23 June 1547, there was a famous meeting of the Consistory at which Perrin's wife called Abel Poupin, one of Calvin's colleagues, a 'pig's snout'. She had to be removed by force. Four days later there was found affixed to the pulpit in St Peter's—at the spot where Calvin usually leaned when preaching—an infamous libel with threats of death, *etc*. It was thought this was the work of a scribbler named Gruet, a Libertine in his religious opinions and morals. He had lunched with Frances, Perrin's wife, on that day and on his way home slipped into the church. When challenged with the deed, he denied all. But this was not very convincing, as in the preceding year a charge had been made against him, which he at first denied, but afterwards admitted the offence. So, according to the custom of the time, he was put to torture and admitted this offence also. Investigation revealed other offences too. Beza tells us that evidence was found of 'an infinite number of other blasphemies'. He was put to death. In the 16th century death was meted out for such offences. It was not only the Reformers who sanctioned such penalties; the same views were held by their foes. Two of the most prominent Libertines of Geneva pronounced a blasphemous book of Gruet's, which was discovered in 1550 (after his death), to merit the penalty of death.

In 1548 the faction opposing Calvin redoubled its efforts. Calumnies and insults were heaped increasingly on him and his colleagues. They sounded handbells outside

JOHN CALVIN

his house in the night; Beza tells us that some of them
openly used collars cut into the form of a cross, while
others gave the name 'Calvin' to their dogs; some even
played upon the name, changing it from 'Calvin' to 'Cain'.
They disturbed the services by their behaviour outside and
inside the church; they defiled its sacred precincts. For a
time even the Council seemed to favour Calvin's foes. A
letter of his to Viret was stolen and his enemies sought
to use a phrase in it against him. They sought to make
him cast a poor reflection upon the Council. He bore this
with wonderful patience. If the rights of the church were
attacked, he was a man of iron; but when the attack fell
upon him, he could show great forbearance.

On 18 November 1548, Perrin was appointed Captain-
general again. Two days later two of his partisans were
given posts of honour in the city. On 3 February 1549,
Perrin was made a magistrate and his associate, Vandel,
was made Attorney-general. These two men now held the
two most important positions and the Libertines seemed
triumphant. They indulged in riots and blows, but the
Council let them off lightly. On 29 March 1550, Calvin's
wife, Idelette, died. On 1 April he resumed the struggle
before the Council. His letters to his friends reveal the
grief of his heart; but before the public he showed an
astonishing calm.

In 1549 and 1550 there arrived a number of refugees
from France, some of whom, like Lawrence of Normandy
and Theodore Beza, were to become Calvin's closest
friends and collaborators. Yes, he had lost his beloved
wife, but God supplied brethren who grouped themselves

94

around him and stood by him in his vicissitudes. The Libertines were quick to see the danger to their cause from these new arrivals. They insulted them in the streets and made a motion that a period of ten years must elapse before they could sit on the Councils of Geneva.

Bolsec was a doctor (or rather, a quack) who came upon the scene in 1551. He arose during a service to contradict Calvin on the subject of predestination. Calvin refuted him with mildness. On another occasion when Poupin and Farel were the preachers, he again interrupted. Calvin came in while he was speaking and, after he had finished, delivered a crushing reply—answering him point by point.

The Council dealt with Bolsec. It decided that he be banished from the city publicly with sound of trumpet, as the custom was. He was driven also from the territory of Berne a little later. He betook himself to Paris. After several changes of front, he abjured Protestantism altogether. He wrote a life of Calvin in which he poured forth a flood of lies and calumnies. This life has served as an arsenal for attacks on Calvin by his foes ever since.

The next weapon used by the Libertines against the Reformer was Trolliet. Calvin had refused to admit him to the ministry and he cherished a grudge. He plotted with Perrin, Gaspard Favre and others in a tavern. Calvin knew what was up and warned the Council of the danger of letting these plottings go on. Trolliet complained to the Council that Calvin had spoken in the pulpit of scoundrels who had maligned the truth in the taverns. Calvin had named no one; so he felt free to quote the homely proverb: 'It is he who feels himself itchy who scratches himself.'

For five months this fellow agitated Geneva. He charged that Calvin taught God to be the author of sin. These men of loose morals disliked Calvin's views on predestination and misrepresented them. The Council pronounced that his *Institutes* set forth the holy truth of God, but Trolliet's Libertine friends secured that the Council give him a certificate of good character when he was dismissed from the city.

Calvin was weary of this battling, but he would not leave Christ's flock over which he was set. So he stood by what he taught in spite of all lies and misrepresentations. His doctrine was not the product of his own brain; it was from the Word of God: and he must maintain it or else be traitor to the truth. So he patiently toiled on. The victory was nearer than he dreamed. But before it came, there was the episode of Michael Servetus.

View of Lake Geneva from the window of Calvin's house.

FOURTEEN

THE BRINK OF HOSTILITIES

THE YEAR 1554 lay in between the condemnation
of Servetus (26 October 1553) and the defeat of
the Libertines (16 May 1555). At the beginning of this
year the Calvinist party met with a success—three of the
four magistrates or syndics were chosen from their ranks.
Indeed there were some in Switzerland who came to the
conclusion that complete victory had been gained over the
enemies of the Reformation in Geneva. As a matter of fact
the dispute had not yet reached its limits. Calvin with his
usual acuteness realised this.

The year was one of ups and downs, and near its close
the Calvinist party received a check—one of the Libertines
was appointed lieutenant of the city. If there was still a
measure of peace, it was the uneasy calm which precedes
the storm. The Libertines showed increasing disregard
for the laws of the city and increasing contempt for fines
and imprisonment. They sought in various ways to annoy
and humiliate Calvin. They attacked him personally, but
especially they sought to provoke him by attacking the
refugees from France. In this year the number of French

exiles in Geneva grew rapidly. They had fled from fierce persecution at the hands of the Duke of Guise. Ami Perrin, the Libertine leader, accused these unfortunates of trea-son—they had come to betray the city into the hands of the Duke of Guise. In other words, they intended to betray their benefactors to their butcher! At the instigation of the Libertines their houses were searched for weapons very early one morning, but, of course, none were found. These exiles had reached Geneva half-dead with hunger, bringing their wives and carrying their children. They were filled with joy on reaching the city of freedom. Now false charges were levelled against them. The Libertines went so far as to suggest that some of them were evil characters. Calvin's heart went out to his sufferering fellow-countrymen, and he was greatly distressed by these attacks.

All through the year the struggle went on. The Libertines sought to have the pastors deprived of the right of excom-munication. They thought Calvin would succumb to their ceaseless attacks and leave the city in a fit of weariness or rage. But he stood fast and pursued his course. And all the time his labours were enormous. His was the care of all the churches. He not only fought the battles of Geneva; he comforted the troubled saints of Strasbourg and Frankfurt and the persecuted churches in France, and carried on a vast correspondence with a host of individuals scattered over Europe on all sorts of questions. Worn out with his toils, it seemed almost as if he would succumb, as the Libertines hoped. On 26 December 1554, depressed and sore vexed with the countless expedients of his enemies and their implacable rage, he wrote: 'If I had the choice,

I would prefer to be burned once for all by the Papists rather than be worn out by these local foes without end and without measure . . . I have one consolation—that soon death will deliver me from a task so difficult.' But the honour of God was involved and therefore he must keep on, trusting ever in divine providence. What could the Libertines do, asks Emile Doumergue, against such an adversary?

The Senate of Berne gave encouragement to the Libertines. It too seemed to be motivated by a blind hatred of Calvin. Emboldened by this support, the Libertines broke forth in open sedition. They began the year 1555 by going out into the streets after supper on 9 January with candles in their hands and singing the Psalms at the top of their voices, but mingling the sacred words with parody and scoffing.

In the following months the Calvinists gained notable victories. In the February elections all four syndics were chosen from their number and there were similar triumphs in the elections to the city councils. These bodies were then to a great extent purged of the Libertines. Various factors were at play in this reaction to the influence of the Libertines, not least the political machinations of Perrin and his followers. He and his party had rid the Little Council of men of independent spirit so that they now exercised almost complete control over that body. But opposition to the Perrinists was strengthened by the addition of French refugees—good men and true—to the other city councils. When the Libertines under Perrin's leadership sought to raise suspicions of the loyalty of these new citizens,

Lambert, one of the city magistrates, reminded him that less than ten years earlier it was Perrin who had tried to bring into the city 200 troops loyal to the king of France!

Though the Libertines had experienced reverses, some of them still held important posts. One was master of the artillery, another had control of a stock of arms, and yet another had the right of access to the clock-tower to sound the call to action. So they felt they could still attain their purpose. On the evening of 16 May the ringleaders met for supper in a tavern. Perrin was the ringleader and he was supported by Vandel and the Berthelier brothers. What was actually taking place is hard to say. Calvin thought that an armed uprising was being plotted; that may have been the case, but it is also possible that the 'plotters' had simply drunk too much beer and got carried away by a lot of wild talk about Geneva for the Genevese. What happened next is clear. Leaving their beer pots behind in the tavern, they set out to burn down a house which they thought was full of armed Frenchmen. Confronted by a servant of one of their enemies, Bethelier threw a stone at him and injured him. Arriving at the house, they were ordered to disperse by Aubert, one of the syndics whose house was next door. Aubert was carrying his bâton of office. Perrin snatched the bâton from him, with the implication that he was sezing power. But another syndic arrived on the scene and ordered Perrin to go with him to the Hôtel de Ville. At this the 'patriots' lost their nerve. The half-hearted and half-sober made their escape down side streets and dark back alleys. Calm was soon restored. The putsch was over, the plot had failed.

But a plot had been made. Perrin had dared to seize power by force. The authority of the republic had been attacked and insulted. Some of the leaders fled the city, Perrin among them. He was tried and condemned to death in his absence along with several of his co-accused. Others less fortunate were tortured and executed. Those who managed to escape continued to make mischief from a distance. But the organised and protracted opposition to Calvin's reforms was over. Calvin gave thanks and wrote: 'Contrary to all hope and by the intervention of God the tempest is allayed.'

It was this event which closed the long period of struggle. There had been two irreconcilable elements in the city. But on the night of 16 May 1555, the Libertines over-reached themselves when they sought to secure their ends by violence. They were 'blinded by their madness', as often happens in such cases. Heated by drink and rage they acted too soon and with too little preparation. Moreover, Perrin, 'the comic Caesar' as Calvin described him, was not cut out for determined leadership. He had done much to stir up the seditious tumult, but then he left it to take its course. Not a life had been lost, but if the plot had been suffered to mature, blood would undoubtedly have been spilt. As for the poor French exiles whose lives the Libertines sought, some slept quietly in their beds while others were preserved, unmoved by the cries for their blood.

With the defeat and exile of the Libertines, a new and final period of Calvin's life in Geneva began—the nine years of triumph.

Michael Servetus and John Calvin before the Council of Geneva.

FIFTEEN

THE ERRORS OF SERVETUS

WAS EVER THEOLOGIAN as much loved and as much hated as Calvin? He possessed and still possesses an extraordinary attractiveness to many; but to the Roman Catholic he is the arch-heretic and to the rationalist he is the high-priest of orthodoxy. Ingersoll the free-thinker took delight in declaring that he had come to believe in a hell, but a hell in which one alone would suffer—John Calvin!

Calvin has been greatly misjudged—particularly on this issue of the burning of Michael Servetus. Prodigious efforts have been made to blacken him. On few subjects has there been so much ill-informed and even malevolent comment.

Servetus, a Spaniard, was born in the year 1511; so he was almost of an age with Calvin. He gave a number of accounts of his early life, but they do not tally. He spent two years at Toulouse in France—from about his 15th year to his 17th. There for the first time he read the Scriptures. Two years later he spoke with enthusiasm of the Bible.

In the following years he travelled in Italy and Germany. In 1530 he was in touch with the Reformer

Oecolampadius, who thought Servetus contentious, conceited, and absurd in his opinions. Oecolampadius tells us that Servetus denied the deity of Christ and used words with double meanings, so as to deceive the simple. This stripling set himself up to instruct men of mature years like Oecolampadius. When he was twenty years of age he issued a book bearing the title *On the Errors of the Trinity*. This was the most heretical publication to have appeared in twelve centuries. Leading Roman Catholics of the time condemned the book—it was the work of a Protestant arch-heretic, for had not Servetus turned to Protestantism? The Protestant leaders—Oecolampadius, Bucer, Zwingli, Melanchthon, Luther—condemned it too. The City Council of Basle forbade Servetus to sell his book there, and its author only escaped imprisonment by making a sort of retractation of his views.

For the next twenty years—1532 to 1553—Servetus played the role of Romanist—a loyal and practising Romanist. He wrote refutations of Luther's doctrine. We find him at Lyon in touch with a group of doctors, and he himself became a doctor to the Archbishop of Vienne, near Lyon. From Lyon he went to Paris. At that time Calvin was still in Paris; he had, not very long before this date, devoted his life to God. Servetus desired an interview with him and Calvin agreed to fix the time and place—at 'the greatest risk of his life', says the Reformer's biographer, Theodore Beza. Those were perilous times to be a Protestant in Paris. Calvin waited at the appointed meeting place but Servetus did not appear.

Servetus dabbled in astrology—losing himself in

fantastic notions. A case was brought against him by the Rector of the University of Paris and the Deans of the Faculty of Medicine concerning his astrological fantasies. Servetus used very intemperate language to describe the University Deans—they were 'monsters' and a 'plague'. But as at Basle, so at Paris, he retracted his opinions to escape fine or imprisonment. He later maintained at Geneva that he was made a doctor at Paris, but the University's records do not support his claim.

After this he practised medicine at Charlieu—at some distance from Lyon—for two or three years. Then he went to Vienne at the invitation of Peter Palmier, the Archbishop, who was a bitter opponent of Luther and Calvin. All this time Servetus was posing under the name of M. de Villeneuve. At Vienne he went devotedly to Mass. As Emile Doumergue puts it, in the morning he would go to Mass and in the afternoon he would write of the Roman Church in his *Restitutio Christianismi* on which he was working: 'O beast, most wicked beast, most shameless of harlots . . . synagogue of Satan' And he wrote this in his rooms near the Episcopal Palace—rooms given him by the Archbishop!

Doumergue gives other instances of his duplicity and says: 'It is difficult to find in history anyone who has for so long and hypocritically deceived the public and even his friends.'

He called his book *The Restoration of Christianity*. All was in ruins. Servetus was going to restore all! As a matter of fact, nearly all the early heresies crop up in this book—Sabellianism, Gnosticism, Manicheanism, and

Pantheism. More than one hundred times he calls the Trinity a 'monstrous three-headed Cerberus' or dog of hell. His Christ was neither God nor man. He had no true sense of the nature of sin. In fact, he affirmed that man does not commit mortal sin till his twentieth year. He is sometimes portrayed as an Anabaptist—a millenarian Anabaptist. He seems to have calculated that the millennium would begin about A.D. 1560. He held the doctrine of the Trinity to be the chief error in theology and the baptism of infants to be the supreme error in church practice. He called infant baptism 'a detestable abomination' and in this connection he called Calvin 'a thief and a robber'. He urged Calvin not only to repent but to be re-baptised to receive the graces of the Spirit. As man cannot sin before the age of twenty, so baptism should not be administered till after that age. In fact, thirty was the proper age for the rite, and in proof of this he quoted not only the example of Christ, but affirmed that it was shown 'by Adam and the law' (Adam was 'born at thirty', he said). The effrontery of the man! He could at twenty issue a book to set the world aright, and then later refuse to admit a man's right to be among the number of the disciples till he reached the age of thirty!

The doctors in France had raised the question—Was he mad? Among others, Mosheim the historian seems to give an affirmative answer to that question. One of his defenders goes so far as to say that too close study of the Book of Revelation unsettled his mind! But he was no madman, weird and contradictory though many of his views were.

At this time also he wrote to Calvin trying to win him and his friends over to his ideas. He pestered Calvin, Viret, and Melanchthon as he had already pestered Oecolampadius. A correspondence of thirty letters passed between Calvin and Servetus. Calvin wrote him some very lengthy epistles and the earlier at any rate were couched in very moderate language. But Servetus refused to be softened; he called Calvin 'Simon the magician'. Calvin at length told him that his views were bold and absurd, and prayed that God would enable him to become more amenable and a humble disciple of the truth. In correspondence Calvin said that nothing but the stake would humble the pride of Servetus, and in a letter to Farel he wrote: 'If he comes to Geneva, and my authority is worth anything, I will not suffer him to depart alive.' Some even of the partisans of Servetus doubt if this was to be taken absolutely literally: but a threat it was certainly. When Servetus asked him for a pledge to ensure his safety if he visited Geneva, Calvin gave him none.

Servetus' book was printed at Vienne. One lot was seized at Lyon, brought to Vienne, and burnt there in 1553 by the Romanist authorities. Another lot reached Frankfurt, but the Protestant pastors there were warned by Calvin—so this lot was seized also and burnt. Another lot possibly reached Geneva itself. Servetus was at Vienne when his book was issued. His secret, so well kept for twenty years, now came to light. Arrested in the Episcopal Palace, he found himself in the hands of the Inquisition. He first of all denied that he was the author (the book did not plainly bear his name).

The defenders of Servetus accuse Calvin of denouncing him to the Roman Archbishop. Calvin's reply was that he had no such extreme familiarity with the Pope's satellites; N. Weiss has shown that this accusation is completely false. This charge failing, another one is laid—that he was guilty of treachery. He is accused of allowing a friend to pass on to Vienne a 'confidential letter' from Servetus. Actually there were no 'confidential letters'; they were already in print—printed by Servetus himself.

Servetus escaped from his detention in France in April 1553. In his absence he was condemned to be burnt alive over a slow fire. Since he had fled the authorities burnt an effigy of him along with his books. If the Romanist authorities had had their way there Servetus would never have made it to Geneva, for he would have been burnt by them at Vienne instead! Servetus, however, arrived in Geneva and was soon arrested on 13 August 1553.

Inscription on memorial stone that marks the place in Geneva where Servetus was burnt at the stake for heresy in 1553.

SIXTEEN

THE BURNING OF SERVETUS

SERVETUS CAME TO Geneva in the summer of 1553. Why did he come when he knew that his views were not acceptable to the Reformers there? The answer is that he was depending on the support of the Libertines whose fortunes at this time were in the ascendant at Geneva. So it came to pass that while at Vienne he was full of denial and dissimulation; when arrested at Geneva he was full of audacity and bravado.

Calvin's position in the city in 1553 was more critical than at any time since 1538. He wrote to Blaurer of the tempests raging on all sides. Prominent Libertines had been chosen to fill some of the most important positions in the city, and the government was now the most hostile to Calvin it had ever been. The Council took away some of the rights of the pastors and assumed these rights for itself. The city of Berne also helped the Libertines. The situation was now such that Calvin's friends were in despair. The notion of quitting the city came to his mind at times and often he longed for heaven—the land of rest.

Yet he continued at the post of duty. After endless

discussions in the Council and the Consistory, he would go home and write consolatory letters to the persecuted Christians of France. They were being hunted 'like partridges on the mountains' and he gave himself unstintingly to help them. He tried to stir the Protestant cities of Switzerland and the king of England to intervene on their behalf. The French king refused to listen to his pleas for clemency. The faithful Christians must go to the stake for their faith. It was just at this time that Servetus, the adversary of that faith, came to Geneva. If Servetus had shown any sign of humility, Calvin was not minded to punish him severely. But as he was utterly incorrigible, Calvin favoured the penalty of death, but not in the cruel form of the stake.

We come to the famous Sunday of September 3, 1553 — three weeks after the arrest of Servetus. The Council had decided that the Libertine leader Berthelier had the right to attend the Lord's table, even though he had been excommunicated by the Church. This seemed a triumph for the Libertines. Calvin would now be forced into giving the Lord's Supper to an excommunicated and 'unworthy' Libertine — to Berthelier, his enemy, the enemy of the Church and the apparent patron of Servetus.

On Sunday September 3, Calvin spoke to a full church. Never was there a day more threatening, an hour more decisive in church history. With the members of the Council seated before him, he defied them all. He declared: 'I will die sooner than this hand shall stretch forth the sacred things of the Lord to those who have been judged despisers.' He came down slowly from the pulpit and stood behind the holy table. There was a solemn silence, which was followed quickly by utter astonishment. Behind the table stood this man, weak, pale, and exhausted, his life seeming only as a breath! With flashing eye he scans the crowd. Will Berthelier appear? No, he is not there! He has not dared show himself. The Supper, Beza tells us, was celebrated in extraordinary silence, not without some degree of trembling, as if the Deity were actually present. Yet what will happen? 'I do not know', Calvin told the congregation when he preached in the afternoon, 'if this is my last sermon in Geneva . . . I commend you to God and the word of his grace.' Actually, his words made a wonderful impression even on the most abandoned, while the good were warned of their duty. It was like a sign of the turning of the tide. One can see, however, how near the Libertines and their not unwilling accomplice Servetus came to success.

When Servetus observed the Council favouring Berthelier, he thought he could see Calvin 'dethroned' and so he grew very bold. He went so far as to ask that Calvin be condemned and destroyed, because, for sure, he 'followed the doctrine of Simon Magus'. Servetus had asked that the case against him be referred to the Swiss Churches. He demanded this course of action perhaps at the instigation of the Libertines. But when the responses began to arrive, they were found to go against the one who had asked for them. The verdict was unanimous: Servetus must be put to death.

On October 26, 1553, the Council of Geneva met. There were twenty out of the twenty-five members present. Ami Perrin, one of the Libertine leaders, made a last ditch effort in favour of Servetus. He moved that the case be carried before the Council of Two Hundred. His motion failed. Servetus was unanimously condemned and sentenced to be burnt along with his books.

It should be noted that this Council showed its hostility to Calvin both before and after this date. There was on the Council a party of the right friendly to the Reformer; there was a party of the left decidedly friendly to Perrin and the Libertines; and there was a party of the centre which was rather against Calvin too. But they could not oppose the united opinion of the Swiss Churches; and being keen to remove the right of excommunication from the pastors, they also wanted to avoid painting themselves in a bad light by setting free someone whom all the world reckoned to be a notorious heretic.

Calvin tried to secure a milder form of death for Servetus—better a quick stroke of the sword than the more prolonged agony of the fire! He was happy to leave to the Romanists a monopoly of the *auto-da-fé*. But the Council would not yield to him.

When Servetus heard of his sentence he fell into despair. Farel came to Geneva, went to see him, and urged him to acknowledge his error. But Servetus recovered his poise and refused. Calvin secured the Council's consent to visit him. He told Servetus he had never sought to harm him; long ago he had kept the appointment at Paris, he had made every effort to lead him in the right way, and he begged him now to seek mercy from the God whom he had blasphemed. But Servetus clung to his error.

The Protestant Reformers—Luther and Calvin and

Bullinger—had not yet seen that the capital punishment of heretics contradicted the principle of liberty of conscience—a basic principle of the Reformation. They held that the church had the right to punish heretics. And be it noted that Servetus held to these persecuting principles too—'Calvin ought to die', he had told the Council of Geneva. In Calvin's *Justification of the Punishment of Heretics,* which was written after the death of Servetus, the Reformer urged that slight errors be borne with, that grave errors be dealt with moderately, and that the extreme penalty be reserved for blasphemous errors touching the foundations of religion. But his *Justification* borders on hesitation. He certainly felt that the stake was logical in Romanism, but not in Protestantism.

An important book on Calvinism was published in 1954 by the Professor of Church History at Union Seminary, New York (an institution not known for its great sympathy with Calvin). In it John T. McNeill vindicates Calvin at quite a number of points. He speaks of 'the well-attested fact' that Calvin sought to change the mode of death to which Servetus had been sentenced. He notes Calvin as writing later, 'I never moved to have him punished with death.' He also notes the attitude of Calvin to the 'Italian sceptics'—Giorgio Blandrata, Laelius Socinus and others. This attitude, says McNeill, 'must be regarded as relatively tolerant for the time, and certainly much less harsh than might have been expected in view of the Servetus episode.' Calvin dealt with Socinus in his visits to Geneva and in correspondence with great moderation. Emile Doumergue thinks the reason was that these men were less of a public menace than Servetus had been; their errors were grave but less revolutionary than those of Servetus, the public agitator. However this may be, Calvin certainly sought to reason with these sceptics, displaying patience and moderation.

A radical professor named Chantre has placed the responsibility for the death of Servetus on Calvin, on the magistrates of Geneva, on the Swiss Churches, on the sixteenth century, all taken as a whole, but above all and particularly on the Roman Catholic Church!

Calvinists such as Abraham Kuyper deplore the burning of Servetus and unconditionally disapprove of it; but they are perfectly justified in pointing out that

> while Calvinists in the age of the Reformation were martyred in tens of thousands (and of Lutherans and Roman Catholics only a very few), history has been guilty of the great and far-reaching unfairness of ever casting in our teeth this one execution of Servetus as an unspeakable crime.

The unfairness mentioned by Kuyper can be seen too when looked at from still another angle. In 1566, a few years after Calvin's death, the heretic Gentilis was put to death at Berne for his heresy. But who remembers anything of Gentilis? All the emotion and all the outcry are reserved for the burning of Servetus!

SEVENTEEN

EFFORTS FOR UNION OF PROTESTANTS

THE THREE MAIN STREAMS of Protestantism in the Reformation movement were the Lutheran, the Zwinglian, and the Calvinist. Calvin's heart was set on a united front. Luther and Zwingli had given little thought to this. Their lot it was to battle and to build—there was little time for anything else. Calvin, however, looked on the divided forces of Protestantism and conceived the idea of uniting them. He did not aim at doing away with national distinctions. Nor did he insist on uniformity on all points. Indeed he showed a marvellous readiness to make concessions on minor issues.

One of the main points of division was the sacrament of the Lord's Supper. Through Calvin's zealous efforts an agreement had been reached with the men of Zurich—the Zwinglians whose leader was Heinrich Bullinger. Calvin went to Zurich and after a few hours' discussion a statement was drawn up which was satisfactory to both parties. So he had succeeded in uniting the Calvinists and the Zwinglians. Might it not be possible to bring in the Lutherans too, so as to form a united front? He dreamed of this possibility and worked untiringly for its realisation, especially from 1556 to 1558.

Unfortunately the prospect of a united front was rather spoiled by the outburst of Joachim Westphal of Hamburg, a rather extreme Lutheran. He stirred up afresh the controversy which had already been in existence in Luther's time. Westphal was annoyed at the spread of Calvin's views and issued a violent and provocative treatise in 1552. He also figured in a very unfortunate display of bitterness in 1553. When a company of London refugees fled in September of that year from the persecutions of 'Bloody' Mary, a storm drove them into Helsingor in Denmark. But the Lutherans would not permit even the women and children to stay but forced all to re-embark. The same reception awaited the refugees at some German cities till at last they were received at Danzig and Emden.

Westphal issued a second treatise as a follow up to the first. Calvin asked Bullinger if he should reply. Bullinger at first said 'No', and Calvin agreed. But Bullinger later changed his mind and urged the Genevan Reformer to issue a reply. So Calvin prepared one and sent it to Zurich for criticism. Bullinger and his friends sent him fifteen pages of comment—they found him too scathing at some points and too moderate at others. He showed a sweet reasonableness in meeting their objections. The changes he made pleased them and they approved the treatise. It was issued simultaneously at Geneva and Zurich in January 1555. The

Zurich edition had at its close a letter of recommendation from Bullinger in which he calls the writer 'our Calvin' and says that he merits 'the universal thanks of posterity'.

In the warfare of tracts with Westphal that followed, it must be remembered that the latter was the aggressor, but it must also be admitted that Calvin used little restraint in his language. It may be said that it was the manner of the sixteenth century to speak so, that he acted under provocation, that he himself bewailed his intemperateness of speech, and that he was accustomed to dash off some of these treatises 'at a gush'—he sometimes dictated to a secretary and did not even read over the copy. We must remember too that he was overwhelmed with work and racked with pain. But when all mitigating circumstances are considered, his strong language is to be deprecated.

In the discussions between the Protestants, it is interesting to note that he distinguished between essentials on which true believers should be firm and secondary points on which moderation should be shown. He always pronounced himself in accord with Luther on essentials and he agreed with the Lutheran Confession—the Confession of Augsburg. He praised Luther and said, 'If he would call me a devil, I would still look on him as a distinguished servant of Christ.'

A conference at Stuttgart was wrecked by the obstinacy of the

Martin Luther (1483-1546)

Lutheran pastor, Brenz, who did not seem content even to make their own Augsburg Confession the basis of agreement. Yet Brenz had been hospitably entertained by the Swiss Churches when he was a fugitive, and had professed warm appreciation of Calvin.

The King of France issued the dreadful edict of persecution against the Vaudois in November 1556, and 27 March 1557 was fixed as the fatal day for these poor Christians. Beza and Farel visited the Swiss Churches to urge them to intervene. They also visited certain German cities to move the German princes to use their influence with the king of France. To show that the persecuted people were true Christians, Beza and Farel produced the *Confession of Faith of the Vaudois*. The princes approved of the Confession, and recognised the Vaudois as pious Christians and of the same religion as themselves. They begged the king to have pity, but he would not listen. Though the purpose was not attained, yet at any rate a measure of concerted action was secured on this matter through the efforts of Calvin and his colleagues.

Calvin continued to use his efforts for a round table conference to secure agreement. The timidity of the Zwinglians and the obstinacy of the strict Lutherans were the main obstacles to be overcome. Yet he strove for it with the utmost ardour. He wrote to princes, he reasoned with pastors. Bullinger felt so convinced of the utter obstinacy of the extreme Lutherans that he wrote: 'I prefer a conference with the Papists to one with such men.' So conference after conference was proposed, yet nothing really came of it. Yet Calvin hoped on and toiled on. He declared himself willing to make journeys if the end in view could be furthered—though such journeys would have been painful to him in his state of health. His efforts were encouraged and nobly seconded by Beza and Farel.

The Emperor Charles V issued the edict known as the Interim in 1548. It purported to regulate affairs as between Protestants and Romanists in Germany until such time as a General Council should secure agreement. It embodied a series of half-way measures and compromises which did not fully satisfy either party. Yet some of the Protestants, including prominent leaders, acquiesced in it. Calvin was not satisfied and it was he who issued a reply. In this matter he appeared as the true spokesman of the Protestants of Germany. Was not this spokesman the only instrument likely to succeed in uniting those Protestants with their brethren who differed from them on certain points? Moreover, he could stretch out a hand to the Lutherans, for did he not teach with them the real presence of Christ in the bread and wine? And could he not also stretch out a hand to the Zwinglians, for did not he teach with them that this presence, though real, was spiritual? There seemed then a hope of success and he strove for it with might and main.

He said: 'What is the great boon we ought to seek with all our strength and with our whole souls—even at the price of our heart's blood? It is even that the church attain to peace and purity. I would journey over land and sea to attain it and offer my life to win it. Oh, I would that all the churches of Christ were united in such a unity as would make the angels rejoice!' Writing to Archbishop

Cranmer of the desirability of this union he said: 'As far as I am concerned, if I could be of any service, I shall not shrink from crossing ten seas, if need be, for that object.'

The endeavour was wrecked on the rocks of the timidity of the Zwinglians and the obstinacy of the Lutherans. It was perhaps in no small measure due to this failure that the progress of the Reformation was stayed, and the Roman Church rejoiced and took fresh heart, so that the Counter-Reformation movement gained ground. But at any rate the blame could not be laid on Calvin's shoulders. He had done his best.

Johannes Oecolampadius (1482-1531)

EIGHTEEN

A CITY OF LEARNING, LIBERTY AND MORALITY

FEW EVENTS IN the history of the church were more fruitful of good than the defeat of the Libertines in Geneva in May 1555. But the full fruits of it were not immediately seen. The ensuing four years were years of transition—intervening between the great struggle and the grand triumph.

These four years were marked, first of all, by the struggle with Berne. There had been an alliance between the cities dating from 1526. Concluded for a period of twenty-five years, it had been extended for a further five years in 1551. It was therefore due to expire in 1556, and Geneva made overtures well ahead of that date for a new treaty; but the gentlemen of Berne were not in a hurry. The affair of the Libertine fugitives had inflamed the feelings of Berne and they seemed to be filled with implacable hatred. Geneva offered concessions, but Berne was unyielding. So time went on till at last the treaty expired — on the first Sunday of March 1556—and Geneva was left without an ally. The city was in grave danger. Farel voiced his fears in a letter to Bullinger in June 1556—fears lest Geneva should share the fate of Constance. That city, after being isolated from its fellow Protestant allies, had fallen a prey to the Emperor Charles V in 1548 and Protestantism had been virtually crushed within it.

Berne made unjust demands and spoke of using force. The reply from Calvin's pen was couched in language calm and just. He was on all the Genevan commissions in connection with this matter, and the most important and difficult papers were drawn up by him. It was not that he loved the political arena. Indeed, he was loth to enter the lists, but necessity was laid upon him. Geneva appealed to the Swiss cities, but nothing came of this. Then suddenly all was changed. Berne made concessions and rapid progress was made in negotiating a new alliance. This was due to threats from the young Duke of Savoy. As Emile Doumergue says, for Berne 'fear was the beginning of wisdom'. Geneva, too, felt herself endangered by these threats and everyone in the city was called upon to attend worship and wait upon God, that he might turn from his anger. The treaty was concluded in January 1558.

Though there was now a new treaty, Berne still continued to favour the exiled Libertines and to trouble Geneva. At last early in 1559 the matters in dispute were brought to arbitration. The umpire, who belonged to the city of Basle, gave decision entirely in favour of Geneva. The citizens were filled with joy and thanksgiving to God. In 1560 a treaty was concluded between Berne and Savoy which gave greater security, not only to Berne but to Geneva also.

A Roman Catholic historian, paying tribute to Calvin,

says that in him Geneva had an outstanding diplomat—
Berne had no one to equal him. His acuteness, foresight,
courtesy, and warmth of conviction were in complete
contrast with the rudeness of Berne's representatives. The
tribute is a just one. Calvin pleaded the cause of Geneva
till the justice of it was made plain to the other Protestant
cities and pastors. His eloquence convinced the lukewarm
and the hesitant. He urged strongly that the unity of the
Protestant cities was indispensable to the security of church
and state.

Geneva had need of fortifications of stone and earth,
for she was in danger from external enemies. But she also
had need to be fortified internally with piety and virtue.
Calvin gave many exhortations to the councils of the
city in that regard. In 1557 he urged the Council of Two
Hundred to acknowledge their faults by which they had
provoked God, to humble themselves before him, and seek
his mercy. In February 1558, at the time of the elections,
he exhorted the people to choose wise men who feared
God; it was a time of danger and they could not survive
unless God was for them.

Though the Libertine leaders were gone, there was
opposition to Calvin's programme of reformation. The
discipline which he introduced was thorough. It took note
of those still attached to the false worship of the Church of
Rome and also of those insufficiently attached to the new
faith. It took note of the lives of the citizens, of the preachers themselves, and of the children. A barber was banished
on account of blasphemy against God and contempt for
the preachers, and for attending Mass. A watchful eye

was kept on those who frequented the wine shops and the taverns. Laws with regard to feasting and conspicuous consumption with regard to clothes and adornments were introduced in 1558. It was decreed that three-course meals were sufficient, with no more than four dishes per course. Not long after, some of the city's highest officials, who had arranged a feast for the Council, were fined because they included a dish over the prescribed limit. The laws of Geneva spared neither high nor low.

It may be noted in passing that in this year (1558) Calvin asked the Council to increase the salaries of his colleagues, but to cut his own. The Council refused the latter part of the request—his high qualities, his unsparing efforts, and the honour he brought to their city deserved some mark of their esteem.

Many cases of wantonness in the community had to be addressed, and they were dealt with fearlessly. With one hand wielding the sword Calvin's Geneva defended the ramparts of liberty; the other used the trowel to build up the edifice of morality.

One idea had long possessed Calvin's mind and he was to see it realised before he died—that was the establishing of an academy at Geneva. He had taught in Strasbourg for two years, lecturing on the New Testament in the famous High School led by Jean Sturm. Calvin's reputation drew many students to Geneva. The establishment of a school in the city would supply a steady stream of ministers for the Reformed Churches and could do incalculable good.

In 1558 Calvin moved the City Council to make a beginning. In choosing a site a concern was shown to secure a salubrious situation and an outlook upon the lake. This concern should be noted — many would not expect it in these men of the sixteenth century. Felix Bungener tells us that 'more than once Calvin was seen, while suffering severely from the quartan-ague, dragging himself slowly over the works, encouraging the workmen, and contemplating with joy the rapid progress of the edifice.'

Le Collège de Calvin.

The statutes governing the Academy were issued on 5 June 1559. They were largely the work of Calvin. The same day in the afternoon the opening ceremony took place. The Church of St Peter was too small for the vast crowd attending. There were present the magistrates, the Council, the ministers, the teachers, and 600 scholars. Calvin, rising from sickness, which had lasted eight months, gave an address and offered prayer. Michael Roset, the Genevan Secretary of State, read the statutes of the Academy, and the confession of faith to be embraced by the students who wished to be enrolled. He also gave the names of the teachers. The Rector of the Academy, Theodore Beza, addressed the assembly, reminding the students that they had come to prepare themselves for their life-work to the glory of God. Calvin closed the solemn and inspiring proceedings with thanks to the Council and a vehement appeal for it to continue in its holy and honourable purposes.

The number of students grew by leaps and bounds. They came from many lands. At the time of Calvin's death in 1564 Beza recorded that there were some 1,500 scholars at the Academy. The influence of this institution of learning was simply enormous.

The city of Geneva.

NINETEEN

PRESERVED AMIDST PERILS

IT WAS A GREAT DAY for the cause of the Reformation when the Academy in Geneva was opened on 5 June 1559. It was in troublous times that this step was taken. The kings of France and Spain—the two great royal enemies of Protestantism—had just signed the Treaty of Cateau-Cambrésis (2 April 1559). The English ambassador at the French court described this treaty as an agreement between the Pope and the two kings to 'join forces to crush the Reformed Faith'. Immediately Geneva made defensive preparations. She inspected her stores of munitions and her supplies of wheat and salt; she distributed her pikes and strengthened her walls and bulwarks. Citizens of all ranks—magistrates, ministers, and artisans—laboured at the defences, but above all they trusted to the aid of the Almighty. The danger was no imaginary one. Geneva was a place of refuge for those who had fled from the persecutions of Philip II of Spain and Henry II of France, and so they hated her. Moreover, the city had formerly been under the suzerainty of the Duke of Savoy, and the then Duke, who was closely related to both monarchs,

Philip II of Spain.

desired to regain the city. Henry II negotiated with the Duke of Alba to blot out the true Christian faith in France, the Low Countries, and elsewhere. Henry sent the Constable of France, Anne de Montmorency, to conclude the monstrous agreement with Alba. The Constable said: 'Geneva is the sink of all this corruption . . . The two kings must concert measures to destroy Geneva.' So the danger was terribly real.

Theodore Beza tells us that at this perilous time Calvin, though he was in bad health, laboured to defeat these plots against the city. Calvin 'confirmed the churches and all the brethren, who, on account of the prospect before them, were in the greatest distress, and was incessant in prayer, imploring assistance from the Lord.' He who sits in the heavens is well able to hear and answer, and to discomfit his foes. So it was that Alba and his royal master, Philip II, hesitated. Shortly afterwards Henry II was accidentally wounded in the eye in a tournament, and a few days later, this persecutor of Protestants departed this earthly life.

The Duke of Savoy kept up the effort to take Geneva. Among other agents, he sent Bishop Alardet to Geneva. Alardet came under the pretext of being ill and needing a change of air. The City Council took advice from Calvin as to the answer to be given to Alardet's overtures. Alardet reported that Calvin had declared that he ought to be put in prison as a seducer who sought to deprive the city of its liberties. On 1 January 1560 Beza wrote to Bullinger in Zurich that 'the wolf or rather the hungry lion which might devour us is prowling before our gates.' A few days later the Council recorded in its Registers the decision that 'by the grace of God they would be vigilant and resist with all their powers.' It would seem that Alardet went so far as to suggest to the Duke the assassination of Calvin; but the Duke, to his honour, would have none of it.

The French Roman Catholic leader, the Duke of Guise, also cherished bitter animosity toward Geneva. So threats from France continued too. But Calvin remained calm.

Pius IV became Pope on 25 December 1559, and took his nephew as his secretary. The nephew wrote to Philip II of Spain as follows: 'One of the first thoughts of the Holy Father . . . has been to blot out Geneva.' The Duke of Savoy asked the Pope for help in the attack upon the city. The Pope promised 20,000 crowns, the use of his own cavalry, and other help if necessary. The Duke of Guise was favourably disposed to the attempt also. But suddenly all changed. The King of France said he was occupied with the affairs of Scotland, and the enthusiasm of Philip II and the Pope declined also. So Geneva was again saved.

In the midst of all these trials and threats, Geneva was being transformed into a city of God. Church discipline was increasingly perfected. It was ordained at the close of 1559 that an exhortation and an admonition be given by one of the ministers before the annual city elections. This was henceforth the law of the State. Before this there had been a system of mutual exhortation and criticism among the ministers. The magistrates and councillors thought this practice would be useful among their own number too, and so the decree was passed. Was there ever such a government as this in any State?

Not till now did Calvin become a citizen of Geneva. The Council offered him citizenship and begged that he would take it. This he did willingly and the Council put on record a tribute to his faithful ministry and abundant labours. It is evident from all this that a new Geneva had been born. But lest Calvin be exalted overmuch, there was given him a 'messenger of Satan' to buffet him: and Geneva was warned that she must not expect to keep him for long. His sickness came upon him and threatened to crush him. This disease—a quartan fever—continued eight months. It so exhausted his frail body, already worn out by many toils, that he never entirely recovered from it. Though at the urgent request of his friends he left off preaching and lecturing when his sickness was at its height, he continued spending days and nights in dictating and writing letters. It is Beza who tells us of this, and says of Calvin: 'He had no expression more frequently in his mouth than that life, as he expressed it, would be bitter to him if spent it in indolence, though indeed we who were strong might, in comparison with him, have been thought indolent.'

On 24 December 1559, Calvin was preaching in St Peter's. The church was filled. He raised his voice powerfully to make himself heard. The next day he was seized with violent coughing and began to bring up much blood.

It was the consumption (tuberculosis) which was showing itself. But soon he was preaching again in spite of the pleadings of his doctors and friends. Just a few more years of toil and witness lay ahead for him.

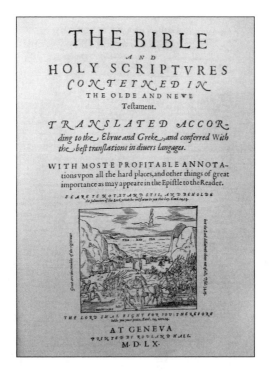

The title page of the 'Geneva Bible'. This English version of the Scriptures was translated by scholars who had fled to Geneva from the fierce persecution of 'Bloody' Mary, the Queen of England. The 'Geneva Bible' was first published in 1560 and went through very many subsequent editions.

Huguenot Church at Lyon, formerly an ordinary house, but converted for
Reformed worship about the middle of the 16th century.

TWENTY

———————

THE REMARKABLE GROWTH OF PROTESTANTISM IN FRANCE

CALVIN'S BIOGRAPHER, Dr Emile Doumergue, calls 1559 'the great year'. True, it was the year of the first *auto-da-fé* in Valladolid, in which Philip of Spain showed his mad rage against the Protestants. But it was the year of the publication of Calvin's final and definitive edition of the *Institutes,* the year of the founding of the Academy of Geneva, the year of the first National Synod of France, which met under Calvin's inspiration. At this very time Geneva was menaced from all sides, and magistrates, ministers, nobles, and people toiled at the ramparts. For the Reformer himself it was a year of great bodily sickness, yet of ceaseless toil.

From Calvin's return to Geneva in 1541 he sought with all his heart to organise the Reformed believers not only in that city but also in France. The years immediately preceding the Synod of Paris in 1559 were years of marvellous growth. Beza, referring to the French king in 1556, could say, 'the tyrant will be obliged to destroy entire towns or else yield some place to the truth.' A year later

Beza expressed to Calvin his great delight at the marvellous extension of Christ's kingdom in France, though he mourned the scarcity of pastors.

In 1557 an infuriated mob set upon a peaceful assembly of Protestants in Paris and seized all they could lay hands on. Beza says that brigands and robbers were taken out of the most noisome dungeons to make way for these prisoners—among them some noble ladies who were to suffer at the stake. Calvin wrote to them in their prison: 'True it is that the trial is great and hard to bear . . . but it is not said without reason that God will try our faith as gold is tried in the furnace, and if he sometimes permits the blood of his servants to be shed, nevertheless he accounts their tears precious.'

The lot of a pastor in France in those days was no easy one. Yet there were many who were willing to venture into the lion's mouth. 'It is incredible', writes Calvin, 'with what ardour our friends devote themselves to the spread of the gospel. As greedily as men before the Pope solicit for benefices, do they ask for employment in the churches beneath the cross. They besiege my door to obtain a portion of the field to cultivate. Never had monarch courtiers more eager than mine . . . Sometimes I seek to restrain them. I show to them the atrocious edict which orders the destruction of every house in which divine-service shall have been celebrated. I remind them that in more than twenty towns the faithful have been massacred by the populace. But nothing can stop them.'

Jean Macard, one of the pastors of Geneva, offered to go to Paris. He was much loved by Calvin, but without any hesitation his offer to go into 'that bloody whirlpool' was accepted. Macard boldly visited the prisoners and fearlessly faced their judges. These disciples of Calvin were cast in an heroic mould.

The year 1559 opened with the signing of the Treaty of Cateau-Cambrésis, in which France and Spain made peace that they might make war on what they called 'heresy'. The pastor of Paris, Morel, wrote to Calvin: 'The fury of our adversaries grows from day to day . . . Some cavalry brigades have been sent against the believers in Normandy who are falsely accused of the crime of treason. The Protestants of Saint-Lô are threatened with fire and sword. I know not if you have learned of the flight of the believers of Meaux; the city has been emptied by the terror and is no more than a desert.'

Eight days after this letter—on 26 May 1559—the first National Synod sat in Paris, 'the heroic Synod'. A preliminary Assembly had been held at Poitiers towards the close of 1558, at which it had been decided that all the churches of France should draw up a Confession of Faith and a code of ecclesiastical discipline. They decided also to meet in the most dangerous of all places, in order to be, by the very boldness of the act, in the greater safety. This notable assembly met for four days under the very shadow of the gallows and the stake. Their secret was kept, and their Confession was drawn up and signed before the people. Then each went to his business—and perhaps to prison and martyrdom. Calvin, on their request, had sent thirty-five Articles of Faith and these they adopted, with some slight alterations. So it was that they finished their work so soon. It has been said—mistakenly—that Calvin did not approve of this Synod. What he advised against was the publication of the Confession. He felt that this would he needlessly provocative.[1] Henry II breathed out threatening and slaughter. He vowed to extirpate 'heresy' in his realm and send the Protestants to prison, to torture and to death. Some of high rank did suffer; but in the midst of his threats he received a wound in the eye at a joust from the lance of Montgomery and in a few days the king was dead. When Calvin heard of the wound he said: 'The judgments of God are a great deep: but sometimes they appear clearer than the sun.'

His son, Francis II, was only sixteen when he began to reign. He was incapable of governing, and Francis, Duke of Guise, and his brother, the Cardinal of Lorraine, took the reins of power. They renewed the edicts against the Protestants and sought to enforce them with rigour. The Protestants had a religious leader without peer in Calvin, but on the political side they looked to the two royal Princes, the King of Navarre and the Prince of Condé, to take their rightful place in the government and resist the Guises who were strangers and usurpers. But the Guises were able and unscrupulous, while the King of Navarre was a weakling of loose morals. Calvin sought to lead the King of Navarre in a right course; his letters to him are models of tact and faithfulness.

Then came the Protestant-inspired Conspiracy of Amboise (1560), a plot to seize the young king and imprison the Guises. It was badly conceived and deplorably

[1] This Confession was reprinted in 1952 in *La Revue Réformée*.

executed. Calvin disapproved of it entirely from the first, but his remonstrances were in vain. The result was to place the Guises more securely in the saddle. Many prisoners were taken by the Duke of Guise, and they went through long tortures, with the young king and his brother at times looking on. The King of Navarre and the Prince of Condé were invited to Orleans to meet the king. It was venturing into the lion's mouth. The Guises seized both of them and Condé was condemned to die. He was to be executed on 10 December 1560, but on 16 November Francis II fell ill, and on 5 December he died. 'He who pierced the eye of the father, had struck the ear of the son', said Calvin. He was referring to the fact that it was with an ear-infection that the fatal illness of Francis II set in.

Charles IX, another son of Henry II, now came to the throne at the age of ten. His mother, Catherine de Medici, now took the reins of power. The King of Navarre might have done so but for his cowardice and folly. Admiral Coligny asked Catherine to give liberty for the preaching of the Word and the administration of the sacraments, but thanks to the intrigues of the Cardinal of Lorraine the Edict of July 1561 was issued, forbidding all Protestant assemblies and public gatherings. Shortly after this, a letter from Charles IX to the magistrates of Geneva complained of the ministers sent from that city into his kingdom, whom he accused of inciting his people to sedition. The reply, composed by Calvin, admitted the sending of the ministers—was it not the command of Christ that the Word be preached?—but denied that they were responsible for the troubles in France.

Catherine sought to establish an agreement between the two parties in the kingdom. So a Conference was arranged at Poissy. Calvin was willing to go, but his enemies declared beforehand that they could not endure his eye or his voice. The King of Navarre wrote to Beza assuring him that he (Beza) would be acceptable to the king and Catherine and the Council. So Beza came to Paris on 22 August 1561. Almost daily he wrote to Calvin. He preached before the King of Navarre, Condé, and Coligny. On 9 September 1561, the great day of the Conference of Poissy came. The Chancellor, Michel de L'Hôpital, opened the session with a speech. The Protestant representatives had been left behind a barrier, almost like an accused party. Beza was their spokesman. In letters to Calvin he had spoken of himself as crushed beneath a load of responsibility, and appealed to him that though absent he might govern him like an infant by his counsels. Now however, he advanced, equipped with the Spirit's might for the hour. First, he and his colleagues fell on their knees—to the surprise of those present—and recited the confession of sins. Beza went on to pray further, and finished with the Lord's Prayer. He addressed the audience with such noble eloquence and skill that he came off indisputably the victor. His implacable foe, the Cardinal of Lorraine, said, 'Would he had been dumb or we had been deaf!' The Conference came to nothing, but it did make the cause of the French Protestants known and clear.

The Edict of January 1562 permitted the Protestants to meet outside the towns and without arms. The number of Protestants was growing rapidly, but their enemies, led by the Guises, were determined to crush them. In spite of the terms of the Edict, the Duke of Guise and his men—on 1 March 1562—perpetrated the dreadful massacre of Vassy. They butchered a company of Protestants met for public worship, killing 60 and wounding 200. The Duke sought to use guile and hypocrisy to clear himself; but unfortunately for him a letter, written by him a day before the massacre, was discovered by a singular providence. In it he ordered his lieutenant in Dauphiny to hang the Reformed preachers. The next day he himself did what he ordered. There is no doubt who was responsible for the strife which followed—it was the Duke of Guise.

Beza and one of the Protestant noblemen went to the French court to protest to the queen. At this interview the King of Navarre took his stand definitely against the Protestants—on whose side he had at a time professed to be—and espoused the cause of the Guises. It was on this occasion that Beza told him: 'It is the part of the Church of Christ, for which I speak, to receive blows and not to give them; but please remember that it has been the anvil which has worn out many hammers.'

Persecution of the Protestants broke out in many quarters, and they flew to arms in their defence. Calvin had always urged restraint, but they could no longer be restrained. So came the first of the Wars of Religion in France. In the battle of Dreux the Protestants suffered a defeat and Condé was taken prisoner. Then at the siege of Orleans Guise was killed by the hand of an assassin. Thereafter Catherine persuaded Condé to sign the Peace of Amboise. By it the Protestants were permitted to live at liberty in their own homes, but not to meet for public worship. Calvin and Coligny and other leaders bitterly regretted the enormous concessions made by Condé. The truth is that though Condé was not so worthless or so base as the King of Navarre, he was far from being of the calibre of Coligny. He had taken an oath to make no commitments without consulting his associates; but he broke his pledged word. Calvin wrote courteously but not hiding from him that the terms he had made did not satisfy the Protestants and that they would retard the progress of the Reformed cause in France. Calvin was perfectly right. It was the first major blow to the rapidly growing movement. Before the next stage in the struggle Calvin had passed from the scene.

Doumergue has a chapter of forty pages on the rise of the Protestant churches in France from 1559 to 1564. The growth was marvellous. One has only to glance cursorily through the pages to see that the organising hand was that of Calvin. No one did anything without consulting him. No pastor was placed, displaced, or replaced without his advice. All paid to him the extraordinary deference of devoted disciples to a revered leader. At this time Protestantism in France reached its zenith. There were over 2,000 churches with perhaps over two million adherents. It was reckoned by some authorities that at least one-third of the land was under the influence of the gospel.

TWENTY-ONE

THE CLOSING YEAR

IT WAS A SABBATH DAY, 19 December 1562, and Calvin was confined to bed with gout. The north wind had been blowing for two consecutive days with great violence. Calvin, in the hearing of several persons said, 'I know not what the cause of it is, but during the night I thought I heard martial music sounding aloud, and could not persuade myself that it was not really so. Let us pray, I beseech you; for some matter of great moment is going forward.' It turned out that this was the day of the fierce battle of Dreux in France. The cause of the sorely tried French Protestants lay on his heart, and from his bed of weakness he was their counsellor and spiritual captain. His premonition on this occasion was marvellous, but not without parallel.

His bodily weakness was increasing, for he took no rest of mind or spirit. He was struggling against a multitude of ailments: indigestion, colic, gout, etc. On 5 June 1563, he preached, but was, Beza tells us, 'amazingly exhausted' by the effort. Some months later Beza speaks of him as having been afflicted with gall stone, and then for a month battling against an attack of gout. Beza later adds, 'I never look at him (and I see him every day) without needing solace.'

Yet all this time he kept toiling on, especially with correspondence. He wrote two very serious admonitions to the believers in Poland, warning against the anti-Trinitarian errors which were springing up there. In this last year of his life there were twelve letters to Bullinger of Zurich, and letters to the Queen of Navarre, the Duchess of Ferrara, the Prince of Condé, Admiral Coligny, and others in various ranks of life. In his last illness when suffering from breathlessness and almost unable to move, he translated his 'Harmony of Moses' from Latin into French, revised his translation of Genesis, wrote his *Commentary on Joshua,* and corrected the greater part of his annotations on the New Testament. When Beza and other friends advised him to desist from writing, he replied that what he was doing was as nothing, and added, 'What, would you have the Lord to find me idle?' He wished to watch and work, as far as he could, till his last breath.

Toward the end of 1563 the gout gave him some respite and he used the opportunity to give his lectures and to preach, being carried in a chair to the church. He even visited his friends to cheer their hearts.

In Beza's *Life of Calvin* we read, 'The year 1564 was to him the commencement of perpetual felicity, and to us of the greatest grief.' Though all was peaceful and orderly within the city of Geneva, the political horizon was growing darker. Beza wrote that, with the return of the Cardinal of Lorraine from Trent, 'hosts of new devils threaten

France.' They also threatened Geneva, which the Roman Church regarded as the source of most of its troubles. For Calvin the end was slowly drawing near. On 2 February he gave his last sermon on the books of Kings, and the same afternoon he gave his last lecture in the College on the book of Ezekiel. On Sabbath, 6 February, he gave his

Calvin preaching in St Peter's.

last sermon on the harmony of the three Gospels. He never entered the pulpit again, though he still tried to go to the meetings of the congregation on Fridays, and say a few words and offer the closing prayer. This he did—in spite of his doctors and friends—because there was no need to speak at length and because he took pleasure in it. Actually, he could not speak at length, because of shortness of breath. Sometimes his body was so weak that he had strength only to take a few steps—but at times he had some alleviation. He knew the end was not far off, and often he repeated, 'O Lord, how long?'

The news of his declining strength spread abroad. Spina wrote to him saying that he had heard that it was only his spirit which remained, his body being only a skeleton. 'Your strength', he said, 'has been sapped by your toils, and what remains is consumed by your care for the churches.' On 6 March 1564, Beza wrote that his bodily sufferings increased during the previous month. On 10 March some of the pastors from the city and the neighbourhood visited him. They found him dressed and seated by his table gasping for breath. He remained for a time without speaking with his head resting on one of his hands—a common posture with him. Then he looked pleasantly at them and thanked them for their visit and the trouble they had taken. He said he hoped to be with them at the meeting of the Consistory for private censures a fortnight later, but that it would be the last time—'I believe this will be my end, and that God will take me.'

The same day the Council of the city, hearing that he was so seriously ill, decided that all of them pray for his health, that the magistrates visit him often, and that a present of twenty-five gold pieces be given him. But he could not be induced to receive it, as he had not worked for it. The very day before his death he preached another grand sermon, refusing his salary on the same grounds. He was able to be at the Consistory on 24 March. It was held in his house, and though it lasted for two and a half hours, he did not seem exhausted. At the close he went on to read some of his marginal notes on the New Testament, and asked their opinions. The next day, however, he was worse. On the 27th he had himself carried to the Town Hall—the scene of many of his battles and triumphs—and presented to the Council the new rector of the school and went on to deliver his last address there, thanking them for their kindness shown in his illness. He spoke with great difficulty but with marvellous charm of manner. 'I feel that I am now in this place for the last time', he said. The members of the Council were affected even to tears.

On the 28th he was present for the last time at the Consistory. The same day Zanchius, in a letter to Beza, sent greetings to Calvin whom he speaks of as 'mortally ill'. Zanchius wrote to Bullinger: 'If the Lord takes away Calvin, what can we say but that he is angry with us because of our ingratitude?' On Easter Sabbath, 2 April, he had himself carried to church, and received the Lord's Supper from the hands of Beza. In spite of difficulty of breathing, he joined in the singing of the Psalm, his face alight with joy.

He was now too feeble to write, though he still continued to dictate. Beza told Bullinger, 'His thin, feeble body is so worn out that he could not endure any remedy. You can understand, my father, in what grief we are plunged here.' On 25 April he made his will. It is full of gratitude to God and confidence in his redeeming grace. He wished to live and die in the faith God had given him. He made his beloved brother Antony his heir, but in the way of honour only (he bequeathed to him a silver cup). To the Boys' School he gave ten gold pieces, and gold pieces to his brother's children and another relative. His friend Lawrence of Normandy was named with his brother as executor. His whole estate was small — the above legacies were to be realised from the sale of his books and effects!

On 27 April the Council was informed that he was sick unto death and that he wished to appear before them yet once more. They were eager to spare him the labour and decided to go to his house to hear what he had to say. He told them, when they appeared that he had deferred this last interview till he had a surer presentiment of his decease. He spoke to them most movingly — of his battles, of his sometimes too great vehemence, of his preaching of the pure Word of God, and of their support and forbearance. He warned them that Satan would stir up wicked men to corrupt the pure doctrine. Finally, he prayed for them and gave his right hand to each. They withdrew in tears, as if each was taking a last sorrowful farewell of his own father.

On 28 April the ministers came to him at his request. In his address to them he surveyed the past years:

> When I first came to this church there was practically nothing . . . All was in confusion . . . I have lived here

Calvin addressing the Council of Geneva for the last time.

in marvellous combats. I have been saluted in mockery on an evening by fifty or sixty gunshots before my door . . . They set dogs on me which seized me by the coat and legs. I went to the Council of Two Hundred (17 December 1547) when they were fighting among themselves, keeping back others who wished to go. When some shouted 'Withdraw', I replied, I shall not . . . Go on villains, kill me and my blood will witness against you and these benches require it at your hands' . . . Although I am nothing, I have suppressed 3,000 tumults which would have arisen in Geneva . . . Be strong and of good courage.

He took farewell of all, and shook hands with each. All were melted to tears.

On 2 May 1564, this peerless letter-writer wrote his last letter. Fittingly it was to his old friend Farel. He had heard that Farel, now in his 80th year and feeble, wished to come to see him. He wrote him in Latin:

> Farewell, my best and most right-hearted brother . . . I would not have you fatigue yourself on my account. I draw my breath with difficulty, and am daily waiting till I altogether cease to breathe. It is enough that to Christ I live and die; to His people He is gain in life and death. I commend you to God. Entirely yours, John Calvin.

In spite of the weight of his years Farel did not let this letter stop him. He came to Geneva and after seeing Calvin and conversing with him, and preaching in the congregation, he returned to his church in Neuchâtel.

On 4 May Beza wrote to Bullinger of the success of the schools in Geneva (with nearly 1,500 scholars) and went on to mention 'the continual suffering of our beloved father'. 'He gave us in life a model of devotion', said Beza, 'and now in death a singular example of Christian fortitude.' On 13 May Calvin's secretary, Jonvillier, wrote with grief and tears of him as 'crushed with pains most diverse and dreadful'. Beza heard him say on one occasion, 'Thou, O Lord, bruisest me, but it is enough for me that it is thy hand.' On 24 May Beza wrote to Bullinger: 'Our Calvin from day to day hastens on more and more to the eternal peace. The day before yesterday I greeted him in your name and I mentioned the earnest prayers of your church for him.' Beza added that Calvin replied: 'I thank those most excellent brethren . . . Lord, keep these faithful servants and hear them, but if it please thee, let me soon be with thee.' Beza tells us that in his severe sufferings Calvin showed astonishing patience and was continually longing after God and lifting his eyes to Him. 'As for us', says Beza, 'we mourn as orphans.'

May 19 was the day for the ministers to meet for their private censures and dine together. Calvin allowed them to have supper at his house, and collecting all his strength, he was carried in a chair from his bed to the next room. On entering he said: 'I come to you, brethren, for the last time. I am never again, to sit at table.' He offered a prayer and sought cheerfully to take a little food. Before the meal was over he was carried back to his room, saying with a smile, 'Though this wall is between us, I shall be with you in spirit.' From that day he never rose from his bed. His face was unchanged: indeed his very looks bore witness to his faith; but owing to weakness and shortness of his breath his prayers and consolations were breathed rather in sighs than in intelligible words.

On the day of his death, 27 May 1564, he seemed to be stronger and to speak with less difficulty. But it was nature's last effort. In the evening about eight o'clock, without a single convulsion or even a deeper sigh, calmly his spirit passed from the emaciated body. Beza says: 'He remained perfectly sensible, and was not deprived of utterance to his very latest breath. Indeed, he looked much more like one sleeping than dead. On that day, then, at the same time with the setting sun, this splendid luminary was withdrawn from us.' A few days later the funeral took place, attended by the senators, pastors and almost the whole city, many in tears. 'He was buried', says Beza, 'in the common cemetery, with no extraordinary pomp, and as he had commanded, without any gravestone.' He was but fifty-four years of age. The only epitaph he would have wished was this: 'To God alone the glory.'

INSTITV
TION DE LA RELI
GION CHRESTIENNE: EN LA
quelle est comprinse vne somme de pieté,
& quasi tout ce qui est necessaire a congnoi-
stre en la doctrine de salut.

Composée en latin par IEAN CALVIN, &
tranflatée en francois, par luymesme.

AVEC LA PREFACE ADDRES-
fée au Trefchreftien Roy de France, Françoys
premier de ce nom: par laquelle ce present liure
luy est offert pour confelsion de Foy.

Habac. 1.

IVSQVES A QVAND
SEIGNEVR?

M. D. XLI.

The title page of the 1541 French edition of the *Institutes of the Christian Religion*. The Latin original was translated into his native French by Calvin himself.

TWENTY-TWO

_____

CALVIN AS A THINKER

CALVIN WAS 'a world-moving force second to no thinker of modern times'; he was 'the great systematic thinker of the Reformation'. Even those who criticise him own his tremendous influence. Emile Doumergue points out that those who repudiate his views are forced to cry out unanimously, 'But see what men Calvinism has produced.'

To know the whole of Calvin—his thought, his character, his personality—we must consult not only his *Institutes*, but also his sermons and homilies and tracts and commentaries and letters. He was the great letter-writer of the Reformation time. Says B. B. Warfield:

About 4,000 of his letters have come down to us, some of them almost of the dimension of treatises, many of them practically theological tractates, but many of them also of the most intimate character in which he pours out his heart. In these letters we see the real Calvin, the man of profound religious convictions and rich religious life, of high purpose and noble strenuousness, of full and freely flowing human affections and sympathies.

JOHN CALVIN

In them he rebukes rulers and instructs statesmen, and strengthens and comforts saints. Never a perplexed pastor but has from him a word of heartening and consolation. Perhaps no friend ever leaned more affectionately on his friends; certainly no friend ever gave himself more ungrudgingly to his friends. Had he written these letters alone, Calvin would take his place among the great Christians and the great Christian leaders of the world.

Doumergue has written a whole volume of 485 pages on Calvin's religious thought. It is not possible in the scope of a brief chapter to survey this whole subject. We confine ourselves to a few points, mostly relating to the *Institutes*. Nearly twenty-five editions, revisions or translations of the *Institutes* were given to the public while he was still alive. When it was first issued in 1536 the author was a young man of twenty-six. Though he enlarged it in bulk till at length the final edition appeared in 1559, there was no modification of its doctrine. Beza tells us: 'In the doctrine which he taught at the beginning, he remained firm to the end; he changed nothing.' Doumergue remarks upon

> the incredible precocity of this thinker who at twenty-six conceived his theological system in a fashion so vigorous, so clear, so profound, so complete, that while during his life of study and rich experience and progress he could enrich and improve it, he had no need of modifying it in any of its essential features.

Calvin begins by striking the note of the song of the angels: 'Glory to God.' This note he sounds all the way through. The first paragraph of his first Catechism—that of 1537—says: 'It is evident that we are all created to this end—that we may know the majesty of our Creator . . . and that we may honour him with all fear, love and reverence.' 'It were better', says Calvin, 'that the world be destroyed a million times than that God's glory be dimmed.' All that comes to pass is for the honour and glory of God.

Warfield says: 'Here we have the secret of Calvin's greatness and the source of his strength unveiled to us. No man ever had a profounder sense of God than he; no man ever more unreservedly surrendered himself to the Divine direction.' He was a sacrifice on the altar of God, 'not only to do nothing but God's will, but to do all God's will.'

Doumergue does not give a correct representation of Calvin at this point. He denies that Calvin teaches verbal inspiration. So does Philip Schaff—but altogether without any solid grounds. Edward A. Dowey Jr. in his *The Knowledge of God in Calvin's Theology*, published in 1952, recognises that Calvin taught the inerrancy of the original manuscripts of the Scriptures. He deplores that Calvin did so, but he admits that it is the case. Dowey says that Calvin never 'implies any admixture of human fallibility in Scripture' (p. 104). As Warfield showed nearly half a century ago, Calvin taught with the greatest strenuousness that the effect of the divine inspiration of the Scriptures was 'the production of a pure Word of God, free from all admixture of human error.'

The doctrine of predestination Calvin introduced merely incidentally in the first edition of the *Institutes;* and, as Doumergue points out, it was introduced for a practical purpose—to cut at the root of the doctrine of works, a doctrine baneful to piety. It may be noted in passing that, in the *Institutes* as in his preaching, doctrine was no mere abstract idea to Calvin – it was to edify the people in the fear of God. In his final edition of the *Institutes* (1559) the doctrine of predestination comes near the end—towards the close of Book III. This in itself is sufficient to show that predestination was not the foundation on which his theology was built, as some have unwarrantably charged. It was not the foundation, it was rather the keystone which strengthens the edifice. To Calvin, as to the Reformers in general, it was a truth not repellent, but rather most sweet. It was solemn and even awesome, but not 'horrible'. (Calvin did not speak of God's decree as horrible, in our modern sense of the English word.)

The root principle of Calvin's theology is the confession of God's absolute sovereignty. This principle puts God on the throne and man in the dust, but in the dust that he may be lifted to the dignity and privileges of the sons of God.

Calvin made an epoch-making contribution to the statement of the doctrine of the Trinity. He secured to the church a deepened consciousness of the co-equality of the three persons in the Godhead. He introduced the presentation of the work of Christ under the offices of Prophet, Priest and King—a most helpful and scriptural presentation. He made a tremendous contribution to the setting-forth of the work of the Spirit as revealed in the Scriptures, so that he has been called 'the theologian of the Spirit'. Above all, he was able, as no other was, to cast the common doctrinal treasure of truth taught by the Reformers 'into a well-compacted, logically unassailable, and religiously inspiring whole' (Warfield).

It is a Roman Catholic historian, Kampschulte, who describes the *Institutes* as 'without doubt the most outstanding, and the most influential production in the sphere of dogmatics which the Reformed literature of the 16th century presents.' It is one who was no Calvinist—Albrecht Ritschl—who calls it 'the masterpiece of Protestant theology'.

Doumergue devotes another large volume to the ecclesiastical and political thought of Calvin. In reforming Geneva, Calvin made it 'the wonder of the world'. Mark Pattison, who is by no means an altogether friendly critic, says it may be doubted if all history can furnish another instance of such a victory of moral force as in Calvin's Geneva.

Calvin introduced church discipline. He stood also for a church absolutely free in its own sphere. He was, says Warfield, 'not only in a true sense the creator of the Protestant Church, but the author of all the freedom it exercises in its spiritual sphere'.

His influence in the political sphere also was vast indeed. The disciples of Calvin were taught to fear God alone and to fear no man. So it was Calvinism which fostered the spirit of religious liberty in the British Isles, Holland and the United States.

In a series of lectures delivered not long ago at Columbia Theological Seminary, USA, it was pointed out that hundreds of ministers were driven from England by the persecution under Queen Mary (1553-58). They went to Geneva where they sat at Calvin's feet. They returned to their own land as heralds of the cross, and, with God's good hand upon them, they changed the face of Britain religiously, politically, socially, and economically, and so the face of America. This influence still lives today.

In our opinion God has given to the church no greater man since the days of the apostles than John Calvin—this 'prince of men', as Spurgeon justly called him.

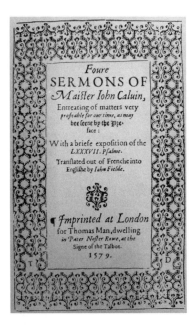

Title page of an early English translation of *Foure Sermons of Maister Iohn Caluin, Entreating of matters very profitable for our time, as may bee seene by the Preface: with a briefe exposition of the LXXXVII. [87th] Psalme.*

TWENTY-THREE

PREACHER AND EXPOSITOR

PROFESSOR EMILE DOUMERGUE delivered an address in the Cathedral of St Peter at Geneva on 2 July 1909, inaugurating the celebration by the Genevan Church of the 400th anniversary of Calvin's birth. In it 'he drew the portrait of the Reformer with careful and brilliant touches.' Calvin was an outstanding man of thought and action, yet above all he was 'a man of speech, speaking steadily for twenty-four years in the pulpit and the professor's chair, sometimes every day for months at a time, sometimes twice a day for weeks.' Doumergue emphasised that this is the true and authentic Calvin, explaining all the other aspects of his work and activities—Calvin the preacher of Geneva, moulding by his words the reformed soul of the sixteenth century. He was first and foremost a preacher of the Word.

Dr Doumergue described in his address how Calvin preached. 'It was in the simplest and most unadorned fashion. There was no pretension, no redundance; everything was with a view to the application, to edification, to substantial results. He spoke in the language of the people,

JOHN CALVIN

making use of the phrases of everyday life, and illustrating what he said with the homeliest similes. It is remarkable how his pages bristle with the popular proverbs of the day, and how dramatically he tells his story.' A preacher like this was sure to be listened to, and that is the first point for an orator. But Calvin spoke not only familiarly, he spoke also with authority. And it is this rare combination of qualities which makes the popularity of his preaching:

> Such is the familiarity and the authority with which the preacher of Geneva dealt day by day for twenty-five years with the most living subjects of theology, ethics, politics and political economy, for to him all subjects were religious . . . There was not a man, simple citizen or member of the Little Council, from the Marquis of Vico or the magistrates to the humblest workman, not a woman from Madame de Budé to her chambermaids, who had not heard enumerated and expounded all his or her duties, the conduct, shall I say, which according to the Word of God was incumbent on the head, or the conscience, or the heart, in all the circumstances of life. There was not an atom of these personalities which had not been moulded and re-modelled by this wonderful moulder. (Quoted from B. B. Warfield's summary in the *Princeton Review*).

Calvin displayed deep sympathy with all human needs and especially with the needs of the heart. His tenderness was well-known to Viret, Farel, and Bucer; it was also known to countless others who sat at his feet as he sought to bring to bear on their daily lives the message of God's Word. He emphasised that if this were to be so, they must have for their master the only master of theology, the Holy Spirit. He was tremendously insistent that no doctrine, no matter how holy or profound, is of any value unless it builds men up in the faith. If it does not, it is a 'useless speculation', a 'frivolous curiosity', 'rubbish', 'a stork's tale', a 'folly', a 'sacrilege'.

Those three close friends—Farel, Viret, Calvin—differed really from each other in gifts and natural endowments. Beza says:

> Farel excelled in a certain sublimity of mind, so that nobody could either hear his thunders without trembling, or listen to his most fervent prayers without feeling almost, as it were, carried up into heaven. Viret possessed such winning eloquence that his entranced audience hung upon his lips, Calvin never spoke without filling the mind of the hearer with most weighty sentiments. I have often thought that a preacher compounded of the three would have been absolutely perfect.

It must have been an impressive scene in St Pierre's—Calvin the preacher standing to minister in spite of great bodily weakness, speaking slowly and with shortness of breath, which were the marks of the ravages of consumption, 'but with all his faith, all his energy, all his passion pouring from that noble head from which no eyes wander, from that feeble breath so distinctly heard' (Doumergue). Truly there was the frailty of the earthen vessel, yet the exceeding greatness of the power of God. The gospel he preached was used to mould the minds of thousands in his own day and of tens of thousands in the centuries since.

JOHN CALVIN

The most outstanding production of Calvin's pen is undoubtedly his *Institutes,* but next to it in importance are his expositions of Scripture.[1] They cover the whole of the Old Testament save the Solomonic and some of the historical books, and the whole of the New Testament save 2 & 3 John and Revelation. It is reported that the Reformer said in conversation that he did not understand the book of Revelation. If he said so, it was a token of his candour and modesty—virtues somewhat lacking in commentators at times!

Calvin was well-equipped for the great task in which he was in some sense a pioneer. He was a good classical scholar and competent also in Hebrew. Warfield says that he was 'a born exegete', and that he possessed 'a clear and penetrating intelligence, remarkable intellectual sympathy, incorruptible honesty, unusual historical perception, and an incomparable insight into the progress of thought, while the whole is illuminated by his profound religious comprehension.' He introduced the modern exegesis; he was the creator of genuine exposition of the Scriptures. Richard Hooker, commonly called 'the judicious Hooker', said that, in the controversies of his time (the late 17th century), 'the sense of Scripture which Calvin alloweth' was of greater weight than if 'ten thousand Augustines, Jeromes, Chrysostoms, Cyprians, were brought forward.' Calvin utterly rejected the often fantastic allegorising which was in vogue before his time and he emphasised the natural sense of the text. He was a 'thoroughly independent student of Scripture'—where the Scripture took him,

[1] These are available from Baker Book House in 22 volumes.

he went; where it was silent, he followed suit. Well it has been said of him: 'No writer ever dealt more fairly and honestly by the Word of God.'

The 22 volumes of his commentaries bear witness to an almost superhuman activity, and of the excellence of his workmanship the recent reprinted edition is a token. These expositions have not grown old. They still remain 'an almost inexhaustible mine of profound thought and wholesome exposition.'

C. H. Spurgeon described these commentaries as of priceless value, 'worth their weight in gold'. He went on:

> Of all the commentators I believe John Calvin to be the most candid. In his expositions he is not always what moderns would call Calvinistic; that is to say, where Scripture maintains the doctrine of predestination and grace he flinches in no degree, but inasmuch as some Scriptures bear the impress of human free agency and responsibility, he does not shun to expound their meaning in all fairness and integrity. He was no trimmer and pruner of texts. He gave their meaning as far as he knew it. . . he laboured, in fact, to declare, not his own mind upon the Spirit's words, but the mind of the Spirit as couched in those words.

The saintly Richard Baxter pays this tribute to the great Reformer: 'I know no man since the apostles' days whom I value and honour more than Calvin, and whose judgement in all things, one with another, I more esteem and come nearer to.'

He had no official epitaph other than that half-line

inscribed by the side of his name in the register of the Consistory — 'went to God, Saturday the 27th'. But in his commentaries, as well as in his *Institutes* and sermons, 'he being dead yet speaketh'.

Theodore Beza (1519-1605), Calvin's successor at Geneva.

BOOKS BY JOHN CALVIN

SMALL BOOKS JUST FOR STARTERS

Truth for All Time
paperback, 98pp.
ISBN: 978 0 85151 749 0
Soft Cover Gift Edition, 160pp.
ISBN: 978 1 84871 022 1
∗

A Guide to Christian Living
Soft Cover, Gift Edition, 168pp.
ISBN: 978 1 84871 040 5
∗

The Letters of John Calvin
paperback, 261pp.
ISBN: 978 0 85151 323 2

BOOKS OF SERMONS

Sermons on the Beatitudes
clothbound, 128pp.
ISBN: 978 0 85151 934 0
∗

*Songs of the Nativity, Selected Sermons from Luke
Chapters 1 & 2*
clothbound, 280pp.
ISBN: 978 1 84871 010 8
∗

Faith Unfeigned
clothbound, 208pp.
ISBN: 978 1 84871 086 3
∗

Sermons on Genesis vol. 1 (Chapters 1-11)
clothbound, 888pp.
ISBN: 978 1 84871 038 2
∗

Sermons on Genesis vol. 2 (Chapters 11-20)
clothbound, 917pp.
978 1 84871 154 9
∗

Sermons on 2 Samuel Chapters 1-13
clothbound, 696pp.
978 0 85151 578 6
∗

Sermons on Acts Chapters 1-7
clothbound, 688pp.
ISBN: 978 0 85151 968 5
∗

Sermons on Galatians
clothbound, 688pp.
ISBN: 978 0 85151 699 8
∗